A Guide for Budgerigar Owners

Hints and Tips for First Time Owners as well as Breeding Information for Experienced Owners of these Beautiful Birds

Contents

British Library Cataloguing-in-Publication Data
A catalogue record for this book is available from
the British Library

DESCRIPTION PARROTS –*Psittacidae*

Bill strongly built, upper jaw bent in a hook with cere at the base ; two toes pointing forward, two backward ; legs remarkably short and broad, covered with small horny scales ; the third toe is the longest and so is its claw; the tongue is thick and fleshy.—REICHENOW. ·

THE Parrot family is found in hot regions, apart from a few species which inhabit temperate climates. Various kinds of country are chosen by parrots for their home. Some of them inhabit woods exclusively, others like scenery varying between grassy plains and woodland. Others are exclusively birds of the plain. Most of them have a hoarse and screaming voice. The food consists of tree-fruits, seeds, in several cases, flower-nectar bulbs, and a few of them also devour insects. For nesting they use holes in trees and rocks, also holes in the ground. One species builds in the open. The eggs are clear white and more or less round in shape. The sexes in some cases are the same colour ; in other cases, of different colours. The plumage of the young is different from that of the adult birds.

Genus Melopsittacus.

The bill is rounded off, upper part with a thin, prolonged and projecting tip, in which are two narrow indentations ; the nostrils are situated on a broad padded cere and are small and round. The base of the beak and sockets of the eye are feathered. The wings are long and pointed with large flight feathers, rounded off at the end, the second being the longest. The tail is long, wedge-shaped and graduated, both central feathers being very prominent. The tongue is short, fleshy and broad in front. The plumage is soft and the colour remarkable for the undulating markings. The sexes differ little, yet quite perceptibly from each other, though the young are noticeably different.

The Budgerigar (Melopsittacus undulatus, Shaw).

Variously known as the Undulated Grass-Parrakeet, Budgerigar, Zebra-Parrakeet, Zebra-Grass-Parrakeet, Shell-Parrot, Scallop-Parrot, Warbling-Grass-Parrakeet, Undulated Parrot, Canary-Parrot, and Betcherrygah (" Good Bird ") in the Liverpool plain and around Bigang in West Australia.

German : *Wellenstreifiger Sittich, Wellenstreifiger Singsittich, Kanarien-Muschelsittich, Gesellschaftsvogel, Pepitapapagei, Undulatus, Andulatus, Augulatus, Andalusier.*

French : *Perruche ondule.*

The Budgerigar is one of the smallest parrots, being about the size of the sparrow, with long, pointed wings and tail, pleasing green and yellow plumage, on the upper surface partly dark and undulated, with beautiful blue spots at the under side of the neck.

Description of the adult male.—Forehead, top, straw-coloured ; on the occiput, upper part of the neck, fore-back and fore-shoulders, the feathers are characterised by regular black transverse undulations on a vividly greenish yellow ground. On the head, the dark transverse stripes are finer ; at the back the dark stripes as well as the yellow stripes of the ground colour become broader. The lower part of the back, the rump, and upper part of the tail-coverts, are beautifully green. The parts around the cheeks and ears like the occiput show, in the upper part, very fine transverse undulations on a yellow ground. Several longer feathers, of a deep blue colour, descend from the cheeks and stand out sharply against the bright yellow throat where the plumage is lengthened into a beard ; on both sides, two of these long feathers each show a roundish black spot at the point. The upper part of the throat is a fine yellow, remainder of under-surface a beautiful grass-green, tending to become yellowish ; the small and medium wing coverts, a vividly greenish yellow with dark transverse stripes following the form of the feather in the shape of a half-circle, as on the fore-shoulder feathers. The last big feathers of the wing-coverts, the last secondaries, and the hind-shoulder feathers, are brownish black with a broad yellow border and similar narrower borders at both sides ; the first big wing-coverts are a dim green with yellow borders like the others, with a blackish streak between the yellow border and the green colour. The remaining secondaries are, on the lace-half of the outer vane, a nice dark green with a yellow border, on the lace-half of the inner vane, blackish ; the ground-half of the outer vane, a bright yellowish green, on the inner vane whitish yellow, which colour is continued as a narrow border till it reaches the tip. The light colour of the ground-half of the outer vane joins the broad yellow lace-edges of the large-coverts, forming a band which becomes broader. Primaries at the outer vane show a dark grey with a narrow yellow border except the first ; interior vane, blackish from the second, with broad wedge-shaped yellowish spots in the centre, which produce on the under-surface a light transverse band, narrow in front, becoming broader at the back. The outer vanes from the fifth to the last show likewise a yellow-green spot, forming a band broadening backwards ; lesser-coverts blue-green with dim whitish borders ; anal feathers blue-green with broad yellowish borders ; edge of the feathers a greenish yellow ; under-surface of the feathers, a lighter green, the light designs are clearly noticeable ; under wing-coverts yellowish-green, partly white at the base with lighter green lace half and broad yellow lace border ; the two longer central tail feathers are dark blue at the base with a green-blue border ; on the under-surface soot-coloured. The remaining tail feathers are a greener-blue with broad lemon-coloured central spot over both vanes and a broad black border at the base of the interior vane, shading off to yellow, so that the tail on the outer as well as the inner side shows two broad slanting blackish-green bands and a brimstone-coloured one, the latter going at an acute angle from the edge to the centre. Under the small feathers there is a coating of down, clear white on the whole under-surface, light blue at the upper-surface, ash-grey at the head and back ; iris, pearl-white or pale yellow surrounded by a broad bluish edge, bill greenish, horn-grey at the base, slightly dark with a vividly dark-blue somewhat glossy cere ; feet distinctly bluish, horn-coloured, sole white-grey, nails blackish (compare page 23 *et seq*).

Adult female.—Like the cock but more or less darkly undulated forehead, the blue spots on the cheek and the black ones on the beard, however, markedly smaller ; cere of the bill from greenish-yellow to brownish-grey.

Nestling plumage.—On the back a whitish-grey fine down ; forehead likewise, upper head and breast-sides when the feathers sprout already appear dark and show a vague transverse pencilling ; the little blue spots on the cheeks are already present, but not the black ones.

First plumage.—On the forehead, upper head and sides of the breast, a vague transverse undulation ; fore-back vaguely olive-brown, hind-back and rump with indistinct yellowish transverse pencillings ; under-surface dimly green. The entire colouring looks much paler than the plumage of the adult, the green and yellow dimmer, the brownish grey on the back, much more striking, bill black, eyes black, feet bluish-white (in the second week the bill becomes a lighter green-grey and the cere bluish-white till flesh coloured).

Length from the tip of the bill to the point of the tail 8 in. to 10 in., breadth of the wings about 10·2 in., wings 3·6 in. to 3·8 in., central tail feathers 3·2 in. to 3.9 in.

The home of the Budgerigar is the Continent of Australia. In New Zealand Budgerigars which have escaped from their cages are said to have multiplied and become entirely naturalised. Budgerigars are always migrating. They stay where the wide grass plains show a luxurious green. As soon as the plains are drying up, owing to scarcity of water, they move to the proximity of streams and to the northern equatorial parts of Australia where the tropical thunderstorms bring a rich growth of grass. Their nature is peaceful and sociable even in mating time. Ever sprightly, they run nimbly on the ground and climb quickly and easily. Mostly their flight is rapid and during the flight they continually utter screaming calls. At other times they sing constantly in a pleasant warbling way. Their food consists of half-ripe and ripened grass-seeds.

Statements concerning the time of nesting vary. Gould mentions December and our autumn (September and October). Probably the nesting time depends on the development of the growth of grass, the seeds of which are used to rear the young. Tree-holes are used as nesting-places. The clutch consists of three or four eggs, of a pure white, and in most cases globular rather than oval. Length ·7 to ·8 in., breadth ·6 to ·65 in. The shell is very delicate and finely-grained with rather deep furrows and small but deep and somewhat angular pores.

The first description of the Budgerigar was given by the naturalist Shaw (*Naturalist's Miscellany*, 1789-1813, and *Zoology of New Holland*, 1794). Wagler tells us that in 1831 a single specimen only was to be found as a rarity in the Museum of the Linnæan Society in London. The famous explorer and investigator, Gould (to whom and to whose wife, particularly, ornithology is greatly indebted in the matter of Australian birds) in 1840 brought the first living couple to England and published at the same time the first information about their habits (*The Birds of Australia*, 1840-1848). He found it in the Liverpool plain in Southern Australia and watched flights at a small stream where they came regularly morning and evening in flocks of from twenty to a hundred to quench their thirst. Before drinking they perched in flocks on the twigs hanging down to the water where the explorer could observe them well and admire their beauty and vivacity. During the heat of the day, however, they kept motionless in the leafy tops of the huge gum trees, so that they could be seen only with difficulty. With the same regularity which characterises their visits to the water they flew to the plain in search of grass seeds, but in harvest time they also visited the corn-fields. In their rapid flight they uttered piercing screams, and on the ground they ran about with ease. Because of their yellow-green colour and their warbling way of singing, early and late, the colonists call them, incorrectly though, canary-birds. Partly in the natural cavities of the eucalyptus trees, partly in caverns hollowed by themselves, they nest sociably, many couples together. The young become fledged in a few weeks. Their nesting time seemed to begin in December (our June), and at the end of this month they had already fledged young.

Brooding finished, the adult and the young join in large flocks and migrate from the South to the North. In the Australian spring (our autumn) when the grass-seeds are ripe they reappear at their breeding haunts, where they separate into couples. In the course of their migration they are said to join sometimes and to gather into really enormous flights with other parrots ; and also to appear sometimes during

7

the migration suddenly in large numbers in regions where they never or seldom appeared before.

Recently Gould's observations have been fully confirmed and completed by a description by Mr. Adolf Engelhardt : " The budgerigar is an occasional visitor to Southern Australia. It is called Shell-Parrot or Canary-Parrot by the colonists of this country with whom it is very popular. One of the favoured breeding-places, the object of my close observation, is Mallee Shrub, a beautiful eucalyptus wood, extending parallel to the Murray, from its mouth to the first big curve of the river. If, in this inhospitable region, after a wet winter, it continues to rain abundantly in the spring—that is, at the end of September—the grass will grow to an unusual density and height. Many square miles, otherwise unmistakably bearing the stamp of a dreary sandy desert, are suddenly covered with the finest kangaroo-grass which, under the influence of the summer heat, shoots up to the height of three feet. The blossom develops rapidly, and about five or six weeks later runs to seed. Long before, however, the pretty parrots have appeared in innumerable swarms, and now they apply themselves eagerly to their task of nesting operations.

"The remarkable shape of the Mallee is particularly favourable for the purpose of nesting. About eight stems grow out of the same roots to a height of about 36 ft. with white bark and scanty tops. Every hollow trunk, every knot-hole, in case of necessity even every suitable cavern in the roots is used for nesting, often by two or three couples together. In a few weeks things get quite lively. The ripe seeds of grass are perfectly suited to feeding the young. Anyone who happened to pass such a spot at this time would be able to catch hundreds of them easily in his own hands. In huge swarms they fly up from the grass when they hear anyone approaching. They perch in long rows on the bare twigs, amusing themselves by chirping songs and unsuspectingly they watch blood-thirsty man raise his gun to let fly a charge sufficient to bring down dozens at once. At last the available seeds are consumed. Perhaps there is also lack of water. The passion for travelling seizes the birds and leads them further. Their next aim is to reach the Alexandrina and Wellington lakes, through both of which flows the Murray before it discharges itself into the sea. It is uncertain whether the morasses there provide them more abundantly with grass-seeds or whether the proximity of fresh water attracts them; but this is the spot to which every year the bird-catchers come in order to lay their snares and to catch many thousands. This, however, only applies to the years with abundant rainfall. But in other years, when the rainfall remains below the yearly average, budgerigars seem to disappear completely. No doubt they then move to the far north where often, in the summer heat, violent thunder showers occur, which, as stated before, completely change a sandy desert in a short time into a grassy plain. All migrating parrots seem to know that by anticipation; for where nature has laid their table, they attend."

At the drinking-places a considerable number of them fall victims to birds of prey, and the overhead telegraph wires cause many casualties. E. Eylmann says: " In the course of my lonely travels in the bush I often watched every day for weeks many swarms of twenty to a hundred birds rushing with lightning speed, fifteen to thirty feet high, crying aloud. In its rapid flight the parrot is not always able to avoid visible obstacles. Among the dead or fatally wounded birds found under the telegraph wires parrots are the most numerous.

HOUSING

THE Budgerigar is a very hardy creature and if accustomed can withstand the severest of our winters outdoors, providing that it is housed in suitable quarters.

There is, however, a vast difference in just keeping " Budgies " and in maintaining them in ideal conditions. They are essentially active birds and derive the maximum benefit from fresh air and access to direct morning and evening sunlight. They can be kept indoors under suitable conditions and will remain fit and healthy if ample exercise can be allowed, together with fresh air, and provided they are kept free both from extreme changes of temperature or badly vitiated atmospheres.

For the benefit of the reader who desires to keep Budgerigars in the house, we would suggest (in the absence of a suitable cage) that a flight or flights of $\frac{1}{2}''$ mesh wire netting be constructed on a wooden framework. Whilst height and width of such flights are of secondary importance, reasonable length in order to provide maximum flight space, should be the aim.

It is better, of course, to keep cocks and hens in separate flights if possible, in order that "bickering" may be reduced to a minimum. Furthermore, when the sexes are so segregated, they usually mate more readily, during the breeding season, than is the case when they are always flying together, also the necessity is avoided of "pairing" birds together for a week or so prior to installing the nest box. If it is not possible to provide separate accommodation for cocks and hens, the utmost space within the flights should be provided. The construction of what may be termed portable indoor flights is not a difficult matter and is advocated by some as better than wiring off a portion of the room, as (if the latter procedure is adopted), the birds may inflict damage to the wall plaster unless such wall is protected by hardboard, etc. The flight should, of course, be provided with a door to open (outwards), in order that admittance can be gained for cleaning out and the provision of food, etc.

Provision must also be made for breeding and whilst the various breeding systems will be discussed later in the Chapter, for indoor breeding it is difficult to improve upon the various types of Breeding Cage which are on the market.

The desirable measurements of the Budgerigar breeding cage are about 3' long × 15" × 15". Such cages can be constructed by the handy-man of ordinary wood or of plywood or hard-

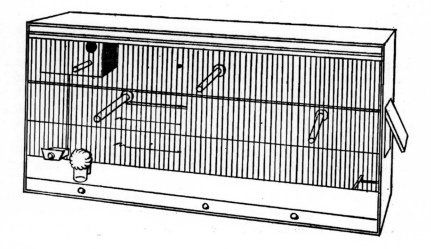

board, etc., on a wooden frame. (See illustration on opposite page.) The *cage fronts* can be purchased to size (or made to order) or the front of the cage can simply be covered with $\frac{1}{2}''$ mesh wire netting, but with the latter, a door must be constructed for access to the nest box, for provision of food, etc., and cleaning out purposes. The nest box can be placed at one end of the cage on the back. It is perhaps needless to add that only one pair must be accommodated in each breeding cage.

Such cages can be placed as desired, e.g. along shelves on one wall of a spare room, or they can be placed one above the other, according to the requirements and domestic situation of the breeder. It must be stressed that under inside conditions as much fresh air as possible must be provided, together with freedom from draughts; it may not be amiss to state that sunlight through glass is *not* good for Budgerigars. Therefore, it is better, if possible, to choose a room into which only morning or evening sun can penetrate through the window if unshielded.

A necessary precaution against birds escaping should be taken in the form of covering over with $\frac{1}{2}''$ wire netting of all window space that will be required to be open to provide ventilation—moreover birds can then be given the freedom of the room from time to time, providing the fireplace is adequately guarded and doors shut, but not, of course, when breeding.

OUTSIDE AVIARIES

These are the salient features which should be given prior attention, viz., construction of sleeping quarters *that are dry and draught-proof* (but at the same time well-ventilated). Plan the arrangement of flights in such a way that the greatest length of flying space is available and, in very exposed situations, some "shield" should be made to afford protection against cold, cutting easterly winds. Whilst Budgerigars have little objection to cold weather, damp and/or draughty quarters and exposure to icy winds are a source of danger to them. There is much to recommend *double* wire-mesh (the wire being fixed each side of the wooden aviary framework) as the perfect deterrent to rats and cats.

Whilst the ideal flooring for flights is undoubtedly cement, turved floors are quite satisfactory as long as the grass is not allowed to become too long and coarse. Ordinary soil when covered with two or three inches of Spratt's Pond Compost also makes a good foundation for flights but in the latter cases, ¼" mesh wire netting should be buried right underneath the soil (and turned up at the edges to emerge above the ground) to prevent the ingress of rats and mice. The covered portion of your aviary can have a floor of either cement or wood, but in the latter eventuality it is advisable to raise the entire structure a foot or so off the ground by means of brick piers, etc., a method which prevents the entrance of rats and mice.

The four most-commonly used breeding methods are colony, flight, pen and cage. Whilst colony breeding is not now practised to any extent by serious breeders, it was a method widely favoured years ago when Budgerigars first became popular.

A simple method of colony or community breeding is to house the birds in a wooden shed, the top half of one of the long sides of which has been cut away and replaced by ¼" wire netting. Removable shutters of glass or windowlite, etc., are placed in position over the wire netting at night or during very severe weather.

Equal numbers of cocks and hens fly together within such an enclosure and a number of nest boxes in excess of the number of pairs is placed in position, *each at the same height*, each nest box being identical in size and shape. No odd (i.e. single) birds are allowed in with the breeding pairs. The liberal supply of nest boxes is to minimise fighting among the hens over choice of nesting place.

With such an arrangement, the birds are allowed to go to nest indiscriminately and it will be appreciated that the parentage of any resulting progeny cannot be guaranteed, for promiscuous matings will certainly occur.

"Colony" breeding has little to commend it apart from ease of management, as it is impossible to keep accurate records. The invasion of nest boxes (other than their own), by some vicious hens (with consequent destruction of eggs and/or chicks, and possible fatalities among the adult birds themselves), is not an uncommon feature when colony breeding is practised. In colony breeding, separate accommodation should be provided for the young birds when they emerge from the nest boxes and can fend for themselves.

Cobalt and Sky Blue Budgerigars

(Both are Cock Birds)

OUTDOOR AVIARIES

16

EXTENSIVE BREEDING WITH SEPARATE FLIGHTS

This method involves rather extensive accommodation if it is the intention to breed with more than a few pairs.

You will require an outdoor bird house, along one indoor side of which are constructed enclosures or pens, in which the nest box and food, water, etc., are placed, the breeding quarters being utilised as a roost of course.

Access by the owner to each of the pens is obtained from inside the bird house, the opposite wall of which can be used for a further series of breeding compartments or for training cages, etc.

Each breeding compartment is provided with an outside flight (generally about 6' long × 6' high × 2' 6" wide), bounded at the end by a corridor from which entry is gained into each flight for cleaning-out purposes, etc. Access from the breeding compartments to the flight is by means of bob-holes cut into the wall of the bird house. One pair per compartment is the rule and thus controlled breeding can be practised and, at the same time, the breeding pairs have access to outside flights with the consequent beneficial effects of fresh air and sunlight.

Such a method of breeding is not, however, suitable for the person with limited garden space, for it will be appreciated that the arrangement of a separate flight for each pair will mean that a rather extensive layout will be occasioned, particularly as additional accommodation is necessary for the young birds when they are removed from their parents.

BREEDING PENS AND THEIR ADVANTAGES

For the average breeder the best method of breeding Budgerigars is undoubtedly the use of breeding pens or cages, within a special bird house, i.e. such as a garden shed or a room indoors as desired—a method which is quite satisfactory especially if the birds are allowed ample exercise in outside flights during the non-breeding season.

Illustrations opposite

(Upper) A TYPICAL OUTSIDE AVIARY AND BIRD ROOM
This illustration of an Outside Aviary and Birdroom embodies the salient features listed on pages 15 and 16. Note the cement flooring, giving complete protection against rats and mice.

(Lower) AN OUTSIDE BIRD ROOM WITH SEPARATE FLIGHTS
This elaborate Outside Bird room with separate flights is the ideal arrangement for an Expert's breeding purposes; it permits of extensive controlled breeding experiments. Note each flight is connected by a communicating door for cleaning purposes.

[*Both photographs by courtesy of "Cage Birds"*]

When constructing an outdoor bird house, the interior should be as light as possible and the aim should be to ensure the maximum of light with the minimum of windows, as too many of the latter tend to create a "greenhouse" effect, thus causing undesirable extremes of day and night temperatures. The interior of the bird house can either be left untreated or it can be finished with Ceilingite or in a flat oil paint *providing it is guaranteed to contain no lead.*

An ideal arrangement for aviary and bird house when breeding pens or cages are used, is for the latter to be ranged along one or more walls of the bird house, the outside flights being attached to the front of the bird house and access to the inside flights being gained by the birds through bob-holes.

The inside flights can be fixed at each end of the bird room running back to front and the space on the rear wall between them utilised for breeding pens or cages. The overall width of the outside flights can be in line with the dimensions of the bird room, the length of the flights being according to the space available and the desire of the breeder. The longer the better, of course.

If in a neighbourhood where cats abound, the birds can be confined in the inside flights at night by means of a sliding shutter over the bob-holes in the front wall of the bird room, which lead from the outside flights to those inside. A door to the inside flights must be provided and this should open outwards into the bird room.

Breeding pens can be made by the amateur but not less than 2' 6" *high* × 2' deep × about 2' wide. They can be fitted with a fairly large door in the front, the nest box being hung on the back of the pen. Breeding pens, which may be likened to cages standing on end, can either be built-in or be constructed separately, the former being the most economical method and pens such as these can be arranged along the rear wall of the bird room between the inside flights at each end, and two or three tiers of pens can be set up according to the space available, e.g. a bird room 14' long with inside flights at each end 3' in width would leave a space of 8' for pens or cages between the flights, therefore if the breeding pens are each approximately 2' wide and three tiers are constructed, the space between the inside flights will provide for 12 pens.

In breeding pens of this description, only one perch is necessary and this can be fixed from back to front above the door in the front of the pen and about 8″ from one side.

Breeding cages are as previously stated, about 3′ long × 15″ × 15″ and can be similarly arranged in tiers along the rear wall of the bird room between the inside flights, and the space between the door of the bird room in the centre of the front, and the inside flight can be utilised for accommodating training cages, etc.

When constructing flights of ½″ wire netting, care should be taken to see that no jagged ends of netting are allowed to remain uncovered. Many a bird has been caught by its leg ring on such projections, with consequent severe injury occasioned through its frantic struggles to free itself. Thin wooden battens are ideal for covering rough edges of wire netting.

The *perching* in outside flights can be of ½″ round soft wood, or natural branches of hazel, willow, apple, pear, plum, etc., can be used but laurel, yew or privet should be avoided as these are harmful. Perches in inside flights and in breeding quarters should be of soft wood ½″ round, or square ½″ carefully rounded at the top edges.

The flights should not be encumbered with too many swings or other obstacles, the aim being to provide as much free flight space as possible, but in outside flights a hanging wire basket to hold green food can be provided. Perches, which should be placed at each end of the flight, should not be fixed too near to the wire netting or the birds' tails will become bedraggled, and if more than one perch is used, the lower should be fixed a few inches forward of the upper perch *so that the perches and birds perching on the same will not be fouled by droppings from those above.* All outside woodwork can be creosoted but birds should not be allowed to come into contact with freshly creosoted woodwork until it is *quite dry.*

Perches should be affixed at each end of the inside flights, in which will be provided seed, water, grit and cuttlefish bone, etc.

Remember the seed, which should always be purchased in sealed packets, needs to have the husks cleaned from the tops of the hoppers; the water should always be fresh; whilst the grit and the cuttlefish bone should always be easily accessible to your birds.

FOOD AND FEEDING

WHEN the second edition of *The Cult of the Budgerigar* was printed, we breeders were still having to feed our birds, in so far as seed was concerned, on what had become known as a war-time substitute diet.

Since then the importation of seed has again been permitted and the growing of canary seed in England has continued, so that at the time of writing canary and millet seed are available in ample quantity and at economic prices. Therefore, fanciers are now feeding their birds as they did before the war.

The staple diet of Budgerigars consists of canary seed and millet. The former is the seed of the grass *Phalaris canariensis*, a hardy annual bearing beautiful flower spikes in summer followed by a fruit which contains the seed that we give to our birds. There are a number of grades, qualities, and varieties, the best known being Plate, Morocco, Turkish, Mazagan, Larache, Tangier and Spanish. The order in which I have written them corresponds with the variation in size, commencing with the small Plate canary seed and ending with the largest of all, the Spanish, which itself varies from a Bold to a Mammoth Grade. Then, as I have indicated above, excellent home-grown canary seed is available. The ability to grow this seed satisfactorily in England was a war-time discovery.

Millet seed is a cereal grown in Europe, Africa, and the ancient countries of the East. It is especially suitable for cultivation in those lands where there is a low average rainfall and the soil is too poor and sandy for wheat or even maize. It is a small grain but little larger than a pin head. It is the seed of the grass *Panicum miliaceum*, which grows up to 12 ft. high and produces its seed in a tuft at the summit of its stem.

The best known millets used by bird keepers are the following, which I have placed in what is considered to be their order as to quality :—

White millet—Italian, French, Smyrna, Hungarian, Manchurian. Yellow millet—the bold varieties, viz. Bombay, Manchurian, Persian ; the smaller varieties, viz. Indian (Kang seed), Italian (Panicum seed), French, Hungarian. Spray millet (in bunches)— French (Millet-en-grappes), and Italian. Attempts to grow millet in Britain have not proved so successful as the production of canary seed.

With canary seed and millet, as with other seeds to which I shall refer later, it must be borne in mind that seeds can vary considerably in quality even though they be of the same variety. This variation can be due to one or more of several causes, including (*a*) quality of seed sown; (*b*) weather conditions during growing period; (*c*) harvesting when mature and unspoilt by adverse weather; (*d*) drying and preparing; (*e*) grading; (*f*) cleaning and screening.

Groats v. Oats

Some fanciers use oats or groats as an addition to the feeding mixture all the year round or at certain times; some use pin-head oatmeal.

The oat is a grain with which everyone is familar and it is quite unnecessary for me to describe this product of British soil. The groat is the oat from which the husk has been removed. Pinhead oatmeal is kibbled or cut groats. As a food for Budgerigars I cannot see any advantage which the groat has over the oat. The birds will quickly break the husks of oats, and as this is the manner in which they deal with canary and millet seeds, it is probable that they will eat oats with greater relish than they do groats. Groats are only made from the best oats, and therefore one can have a confidence when using them which cannot exist with some oats, though this position can easily be overcome by only buying the very best oats. Newly harvested oats have more sap in the grain than have groats, and would, therefore, probably be more appreciated by the birds. White groats are better than brown groats. Groats and oatmeal have an advantage over oats when mixing cod-liver oil with the seed, as I shall explain later.

It is a mistake to exercise false economy when purchasing seed, and I warn my readers against the dangerous practice of obtaining inferior qualities merely because they are cheaper. Generally speaking, the most expensive grades are the best.

Only by experience can fanciers learn to appreciate good quality seed by appearance, cleanliness, plumpness, sound kernels (which is very important), and sweet taste, and, therefore, they should always purchase their supplies from reputable firms who have a thorough understanding of the Budgerigar's needs.

On the next page an analysis is given of the seeds used in the feeding of Budgerigars, and of other products for comparison purposes. These figures given can be accepted as being approximately correct, although analyses are subject to some variation in accordance with the actual quality of the seeds.

Carbohydrates provide heat, force and vital energy by their oxidation or burning up within the body.

Proteids (albuminoids) form tissue and build up and repair wastage of body substance.

Fats provide heat and energy.

The mineral substances are bone providing, and they also supply chemical salts to the glands, the blood, and the digestive fluids of

	Proteids (Albuminoids)	Fats or Oils	Carbohydrates	Salts and Minerals
Canary Seed	13·5	4·9	51·6	2·1
Rape Seed	19·4	40·5	10·2	3·9
Hemp Seed	10·0	21·0	45·0	2·0
Maw Seed	17·5	40·3	12·2	5·8
Niger Seed	17·5	32·7	15·3	7·0
Millet Seed.. ..	11·3	4·0	60·0	3·0
Sunflower Seed ..	16·0	21·5	21·4	2·6
Linseed	25·0	40·0	18·0	5·7
Peas	22·0	2·0	53·0	2·4
Beans	24·0	1·4	44·0	3·6
Tares	25·0	1·5	46·0	3·0
Lentils	29·0	1·5	44·0	2·3
Wheat	11·0	2·0	70·0	1·7
Barley	10·0	2·4	70·0	2·0
Oats	12·0	6·0	62·0	3·0
Maize	10·0	7·0	65·0	1·7
Rice	5·0	0·5	83·0	0·5
Green Vegetables	2·0	0·5	4·0	0·7

the body. Then there are the vitamins, but these I will deal with separately later.

The Balanced Ration

The perfectly balanced ration for a Budgerigar would consist of just the correct proportion of proteids, carbohydrates, fats, minerals, and salts to fulfil the bodily requirements of the bird. Experience has taught us, particularly during the war, that analyses are not by any means a certain guide. For example, the differences in the percentages between oats and canary seed are not, prima facie, sufficient to indicate any great difference in nutritional value. Yet oats, useful as some consider them to be as an auxiliary food, are incomparable with canary seed in so far as Budgerigar feeding is concerned. This may be due to variation in the qualities, as apart from the quantities, of the constituents of the two grains. For instance, the protein in canary seed might be superior to the protein in oats. Be this as it may, our birds certainly do much better when canary seed alone, or millet seed alone or when mixed together, is the staple diet.

More Research Needed

There has not been carried out with Budgerigar feeding extensive experiments such as there have been in connection with poultry culture, and we have still to a great extent to rely on the " trial and error " principle, and feed our birds on those seeds, etc., and in those proportions which have given to others and ourselves satisfactory results, and on the Budgerigar's natural instinct to eat from the food we place before it just sufficient of each kind to satisfy its system's demands. There is here provided a field for the experimentalist in the science of nutrition.

The purpose of food is to develop growth in the young, and in birds of all ages maintain and repair body substance and produce heat and energy ; and the perfect diet must necessarily be so constituted that it meets all these requirements. It should be so flexible that it can be changed suitably in accordance with the particular seasons of the year, the facility or lack of facility for exercise, the condition of the Budgerigars at stated times—for instance, whether they are too fat or too thin, or moulting—and particularly should it be adjusted within reasonable limits when the parent birds are feeding youngsters.

In actual practice with this species we are somewhat limited as to the food which they will eat, there being many additions which we could make to their dietary if they would co-operate with us by consuming them. But I have found in my experience that Budgerigars are somewhat particular as to what they will eat and what they will not eat. I always argue, however, that birds and animals will naturally usually select those things, if available, which are good for them and that we need not worry unduly because of our inability to induce them to experiment with foods which we rightly or wrongly think would be to their benefit ; and it is gratifying to realise that a comparatively simple diet is sufficient to keep Budgerigars in good health and condition.

I have already said that in normal times their staple food consists of canary seed and millet, and I have as yet been unable to improve upon a mixture consisting of equal parts of millet and canary seed.

If economy in feeding has to be considered, as it has had to be during and since the war, then the proportion of millet can be divided into two parts of white millet and one part of yellow millet, because the yellow is considerably cheaper than the white. Otherwise there is no objection to using white millet only.

23

Millet sprays are now very expensive. Apart from this it is quite a good practice—though not essential—to hang them up in the cages or aviaries say once per week. They are particularly beneficial to the youngsters in the nursery. The seed of French millet spray is of high quality; in addition, the birds particularly enjoy picking it, which activity I am sure acts as a tonic.

Vitamins

Before I pass along to the subjects of green foods, roots, and possible suitable additions to the dietary during the breeding season, I think it will be helpful to my readers, if I say here something about the important question of vitamins, the study of which is a science and has undoubtedly proved to be of tremendous importance in the feeding of human beings, animals, and birds. These vitamins are elements in food which undoubtedly have a very important bearing upon health and which should be provided in ample quantity not only with a view to maintaining physical condition but also as a preventative of disease. The vitamins consist of the following :—

VITAMIN A (Fat Soluble)—assists growth and increases stamina and the resistance to disease.

VITAMIN B (Water Soluble)—its presence strengthens the nervous system and is therefore conducive to good health generally. Its deficiency is a common cause of neuritis and various nerve disorders.

VITAMIN C (Anti-Scorbutic)—its deficiency causes skin diseases.

VITAMIN D (Anti-Rachitic)—assists in the formation of bone and its absence causes rickets.

VITAMIN E—prevents sterility and increases fertility.

These vitamins in varying quantities are in all the foods which we give to Budgerigars.

The most important vitamins to the Budgerigar keeper are Vitamins A and D, which are contained in cod liver oil. Because of the probability that the ordinary foods do not provide a sufficiency of Vitamins A and D, many of us are of the opinion that cod liver oil of the best quality is a most valuable auxiliary food (I look upon it as a food and not as a medicine).

How to give Cod Liver Oil

The best method of giving cod liver oil is to include one teaspoonful of oil with each pint of seed. It should be well mixed into the seed with the hands until he who is doing the mixing is satisfied that it is fully distributed. The job should be done thoroughly in order to prevent some parts of the mixture carrying more of the oil on the husks than other parts.

At Lintonholme we use cod liver oil all the year round except when the birds are breeding. It is particularly beneficial during the cold days of winter when there is at times an almost complete absence of sunshine. During the summer when the sun is shining daily and when good health can be maintained more easily than at other periods of the year, vitamin deficiency is not so likely to occur and cod liver oil is therefore not then so necessary as on other occasions.

I do believe that a course of cod liver oil prior to birds commencing to breed not only strengthens them for the task which is before them but also puts them into such a state of health that egg binding is not likely to occur.

I have stated above that cod liver oil should be given in the proportion of one teaspoonful to one pint of seed. The usual method is simply to put the oil in the ordinary canary seed-millet mixture and distribute it by hand, mixing so thoroughly that every bit of seed becomes coated with the oil.

An alternative way of administering cod liver oil is to mix it with a de-husked grain. (Groats, when we are permitted to use them, are particularly suitable for the purpose). The advantage of this system is that the whole of the oil is absorbed, whereas without doubt when C.L.O. is mixed into canary seed or millet some oil is lost when the birds de-husk the seed. It is essential that only cod liver oil of the very best quality and highest vitamin content should be used.

Halibut liver oil is many more times richer in Vitamins A and D than is cod liver oil and, therefore, of course, a much smaller quantity will give equal results. But for this reason in itself it is not so good for our purpose as is cod liver oil as one cannot distribute very small quantities of halibut liver oil over a pint or more of seed.

I am convinced that green foods or roots are most beneficial to Budgerigars, though not so *essential* as at one time we all thought. If possible they should be provided daily during the breeding season and *at least* three times per week when the birds are not engaged with parental duties.

The richer the soil on which the greens are grown the more nutritious they will be. They should not be gathered at the roadside or in fields which can possibly have been fouled.

As autumn approaches the early wild plants, particularly following a season of extreme heat and dryness, lose their feeding value, and it is then advisable to discontinue using them and commence to give cultivated greens or roots.

Useful Seeding Grasses

When seeding grasses are available they are a valuable addition to the Budgerigar's dietary—in fact, the best of all green foods—particularly for adults rearing chicks, and youngsters after they leave the nest. They possess desirable properties additional to those contained in dry seeds. The birds eat them with great relish.

Common chickweed is well known to everyone who owns a garden. In addition to possessing the other properties for which greens are valuable it is said to be rich in Vitamin E, and for this reason it is claimed that it increases fecundity. It grows profusely as a weed, and there is usually little difficulty in gathering ample quantities of it.

The common dandelion is an admirable tonic, but I do not think it is a green which should be given too frequently.

Groundsel, like chickweed, is easy to find and is given to Budgerigars by some fanciers. Others, however, speak disparagingly of it and consider that it is inclined to cause diarrhoea. As there are plenty of other greens to be had for the gathering, I do not use groundsel.

The birds like plantain, and it is a good food. Against it there cannot be made the same charge which is levelled against groundsel, inasmuch as it is inclined to be slightly astringent in its action.

Shepherd's Purse a Tonic

Long-leaf plantain is also a useful green, as is common shepherd's purse. This plant is both a tonic and an astringent. On the first signs of scours in a rabbit many practical breeders of these animals give to the sufferer a feed of shepherd's purse, and a complete cure is often soon effected. Budgerigars thoroughly enjoy picking the seeds from this plant.

Of course I could go on and on describing wild greens which can be given to Budgerigars—there are so many of them—but I think I have named sufficient to give my readers ample choice, in addition to which they might consider, if they wish, those other weeds favoured by rabbit breeders, who as a body have studied the green food question seriously, viz. common burnet, hogweed, clover, coltsfoot, cleavers (also known as cly, sweetheart and goose grass, and which is beloved of geese and turkeys), common nipplewort, and sow thistle.

Sketch of the finished appearance of the breeding aviary from the constructional details set out in the blueprint included in this book

THE STANDARD BUDGERIGAR SHOW CAGE

But, after all, it is advisable for the fancier who is not a botanist to confine his attentions to those plants with the appearance and value of which he is familiar, because there are some wild greens which are definitely dangerous to birds and animals, well-known examples of which are arum (cuckoo-pint), anemone (windflower), autumn crocus, belladonna (nightshade), white bryony, celandine, figwort, fool's parsley, hemlock, etc.

When suitable wild green food is unobtainable the Budgerigar breeder must turn to cultivated greens and roots. In this category very popular with many fanciers is the lettuce. Personally I think a fresh lettuce is a useful food, but particular care should be taken not to put more into the aviary than will be quickly eaten. When once lettuce leaves begin to turn yellow in my view they can simultaneously commence to be unsuitable as food.

I have found nothing superior to perpetual spinach as a cultivated green, and we always have some growing in our garden. In fact, in recent years we have used this exclusively when spring and early-summer greens, particularly seeding grasses, have been no longer available.

Chicory is another good green-food.

Some breeders give to their birds those green vegetables which they eat themselves, cabbage, brussels sprouts, kale, watercress, celery, etc.

Winter Substitutes

In the winter many fanciers substitute the wild greens of summer by putting in the aviaries apples, beetroot, swedes, or carrots. Of these I prefer carrots, which I think combine all the essential requirements.

Young carrots, cut into four by slicing down the middle, are readily eaten by Budgerigars when once they have got used to them, and their composition is such that they balance greenfood deficiency when wild plants are unobtainable; and they are rich in vitamins.

Differences of opinion exist with regard to the value of green foods and roots as an auxiliary diet. Although it is unwise to give these products too extensively, I think the majority of keepers consider that *reasonable* supplies of them are beneficial to the health of their birds. There are some fanciers who only supply these foods occasionally, and there are a small minority who do not utilise them at all.

My own view is that the *lavish* use of greens is undesirable. They are not so important as the staple diet of canary seed and millet.

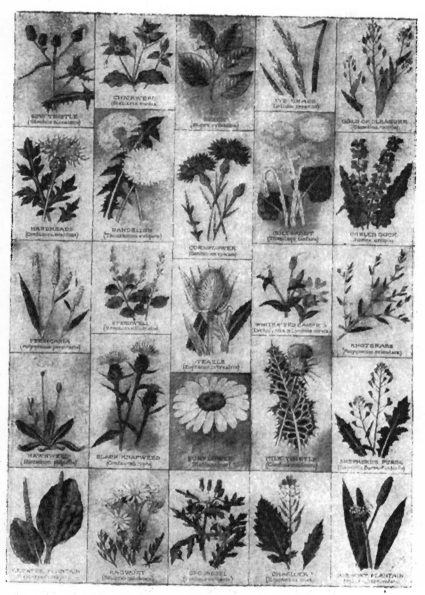

A Selection of Wild Foods Suitable for Budgerigars.

A little at a time given more regularly is, in my opinion, preferable to giving greens or roots infrequently, and then in large quantities, with the result that the birds literally gorge themselves, which can be particularly dangerous if they are feeding chicks.

Greenfoods or roots given in a sensible way do serve a valuable purpose, because they contain a relatively high percentage of desirable vegetable salts and vitamins and they have a cooling effect on the system. They also counteract obesity.

Dried Grass Offered

I have said above that I do not consider greens to be so essential as at one time we all thought they were. During the war when my aviary attendant was away on service and I was every day crowding two hours into one, I often found I could not give greens for quite lengthy periods, and yet the fact remains that although the stock were being mainly fed on a substitute diet they did not apparently suffer. I do not say that they would not have been better if they had been getting greens frequently, but there were certainly no untoward results. Nevertheless, I became rather worried about the absence of green foods and I found a very good substitute in dried grass.

I mixed the dried grass into the soaked seed, to which it adhered and in that way the birds got a proportion of it. Some, of course, was cast away with the husks.

Simple Diet Best

So far I have dealt with the simplest form of feeding Budgerigars, having described a dietary which is capable alone of keeping our birds in good health all the year round ; and I have, after much experimenting and a lot of study, almost come to the conclusion that, broadly speaking, Budgerigars do best on a comparatively simple diet without anything in the nature of what can be termed " fancy " feeding. And yet there are some additional foods which can be utilised at different seasons with considerable advantage, judging by the results reported to me by other breeders.

Sprouted seeds are one of the most popular of the auxiliary foods. Oats, wheat, or a mixture of the seeds suitable for Budgerigars are sprouted in one of the several excellent mechanical sprouters which are frequently advertised. The appearance of the sprout on a seed follows germination, which changes the food value of the seed. Canary seed and millet can be sprouted similarly.

Another method of obtaining the beneficial effects which are to be derived from grain in which germination has commenced is to take a quantity of one variety of seed, or of the entire mixture, place it in a bucket, cover it with water and leave it over-night. Next morning transfer the seed to another bucket in which holes have been pierced in the bottom. Put this on a wooden frame above a third bucket, into which the water gradually drains away from the seed, leaving the latter just moist before it is placed in the pots in each aviary.

Valuable Diastase

When grain is placed in water germination commences within one hour, and germination produces diastase, a nitrogenous ferment created from the digestive juices of the plant acting on the starch of the seed. Diastase dissolves starch into dextrine, which is easily digestible and quickly assimilated by the blood-stream. Dextrine is the basis of many proprietary baby and invalid foods. I am given to understand that diastase is so powerful that one part will dissolve or pre-digest 2,000 parts of starch, and one part of germinated grain will produce enough diastase to convert the starch in six times as much grain into sugar.

The value of the various malt products advertised rests, I am told, on the fact that malt, which is germinated barley dried and ground, is rich in diastase.

I think my readers who have made use of either soaked or sprouted seed will have observed how the parent birds when feeding chicks will show a preference for it over the seed in the hoppers, which would point to the fact that it provides something which is desirable.

Bread and milk placed in little pots in the aviaries occupied by birds which are rearing chicks has been often advocated by writers in the cage-bird Press. The bread used for the purpose should be either wholemeal bread or one of the special Budgerigar breads which are advertised. White bread is not so suitable.

No doubt some of the special conditioners which are on the market have their respective values, and I know of one breeder who rears a large number of youngsters every season who gives broken puppy biscuits as an auxiliary food !

I have referred to those additions to the staple diet which I have either made use of myself or had recommended to me, and I must now leave it to my reader's own experience to guide him as to which system to adopt ; but I warn him not to be frequently changing his feeding procedure and carrying out experiments with foods, possibly to his ultimate loss. A good, well-established simple feeding routine is preferable to one whose principal feature is its irregularity.

Nothing is more important in the feeding of Budgerigars than the provision of a suitable grit, which should be of such a nature that not only does it serve to grind the food and aid the process of digestion but also provides certain essential mineral constituents of which calcium or lime is the most important. Lack of calcium is injurious to the general health of any living thing and a deficiency of this mineral will cause weakness in bone formation. Other mineral substances which the system of a Budgerigar demands are iron, iodine, carbon, magnesia, etc.

I believe some of the grits advertised are as near ideal for the purpose as man can make them. Personally so important do I consider the provision of lime that I use a grit containing 90 per cent. of it.

Old mortar is valuable for the same reason, and it is undoubtedly because of its high calcium content, plus certain helpful salts, that cuttle fish bone is popular with most cage bird keepers.

It is claimed by many authorities that sea-sand will serve all the needs for which grit is used, but personally, whilst I agree that it possesses valuable properties, I do not think it can, alone, provide as much calcium as is required. It is essential that the grit should be finely ground, so that there is no danger of its injuring the birds' intestines as it can do if it contains large sharp-edged pieces.

Not a bad practice is to provide both sea-sand and a grit consisting almost entirely of crushed limestone. Some fanciers use sea-sand as a floor covering in the houses and cages. I do not use any floor covering.

Unless a bird is ailing, generally speaking I do not advocate the use of drugs and stimulants. If Budgerigars come from healthy stock and are correctly fed and well managed they should retain good health without the aid of any artificial treatment. The only exception to this rule which I might countenance is in the case of a suitable tonic, a course of which can undoubtedly be beneficial, for instance, preparatory to the breeding season, during the moult, and in the case of those birds which are being prepared for exhibition.

How to give Tonics

Most fanciers give tonics in the drinking water, but I think this is a mistake. Owing to the fact that Budgerigars drink so sparingly one cannot administer to them by this method a sufficiency of any tonic to do any particular good. A much better plan is to give it by means of the millet spray or ordinary seed. A good system is to put a sufficiency of the tonic into cold water and steep the millet spray or seed in it overnight, giving it wet to the birds next morning.

It is essential that Budgerigars should always have food in front of them. Unlike poultry and pigeons they cannot safely be given a meal in a morning and another in the evening—just sufficient for them to eat up on each occasion. They must be able to eat when they want to eat. In actual practice it will be found that they themselves fix more or less regular mealtimes, their largest feed being before they retire to their perches for the night.

If a Budgerigar is deprived of food for any length of time it displays signs of distress, and it will quickly succumb if seed is not provided before it is too late. I have known pigeons live for days when through accident there has not been any corn available to them, whereas a Budgerigar cannot last twelve hours. Therefore the only safe course to pursue is to be meticulous in carrying out the injunction never to have the food pots or hoppers empty.

During the war when canary and millet were unobtainable except in comparatively small quantities and at a fantastic cost (prices rose to over £100 per cwt.) substitute diets had to be found. Great ingenuity was displayed, and had it not been for the acumen shown by fanciers in those terrible years, the Budgerigar Fancy as we know it to-day would not now exist. These substitute diets contained such seeds as persicaria (Red Shank) and Buckwheat, which proved to be about the best of the many wild seeds which were tried.

It says much for the determination and fortitude of breeders that they did overcome the crisis, and although many Budgerigars died the strains were kept intact.

Keeping the Birds Healthy

BUDGERIGARS are subject to comparatively few diseases. The main object should be to keep them in good health by following carefully the directions given in the previous chapters. Prevention is better than cure.

Budgerigars will stand all temperatures occurring in our climate. They will live comfortably the year through in the open air or they may be allowed to winter in unheated or slightly heated rooms.

What they cannot endure is an abrupt change of temperature, caused by the entrance of damp or cold air currents while the room is being cleaned. Bad results will also follow from the effects of over-heating, dark rooms, foul air, tobacco smoke, damp walls and floors.

If Budgerigars are to thrive their abode must be bright, sunny, and light, and they must have fresh, pure air.

During the warm season it is easy to provide for ventilation by opening the windows. The question becomes more difficult in the winter if the birds are kept in heated rooms. In living-rooms cages must be hung so that they are secure from darkness and stuffiness. Ventilation is provided by opening the windows in the adjoining room and keeping them open for a long time, because ventilation is only very slow. If the windows of the room where the cages are must be opened, the cages should be removed from the window as far as possible and covered by hanging a cloth over them. In heated birdrooms the air is also renewed from an adjoining room, by means of stoves provided with a ventilating apparatus or by special pipes for the intake and outlet of air, the fixing-up of which must be carried out by proper workmen. Care must be taken that the entrance of fresh air and the elimination of impure air is not attended with draught and great changes of temperature. The heating of birdrooms in which Budgerigars are kept causes no difficulties. An air temperature of 60 to 77 degrees is healthy. Stoves which cannot be closed and those which are liable to become red-hot are unsuitable for birdrooms. Some stoves, which emit considerable heat, have to be provided with iron screens.

BATHING

Budgerigars are evidently not as fond of bathing as most other birds, although they must be given an opportunity to do so now and then. Young Budgerigars bathe more frequently than old ones. Care must be taken that the water spilt in bathing does not soak the floor covering. The simplest bathing vessel for Budgerigars that are kept in cages is the little bathing cabin (Fig. 22) to be hung outside the open door of the cage. In birdrooms a flat bathing vessel is put into a large zinc tray which receives the spilt water. The height of the water in the bath should be about an inch.

When Budgerigars are only just fledged no bathing facilities should be given. In gauging the temperature of the bathing water the same care must be taken as in the case of drinking water. Budgerigars prefer to damp their plumage in wet branches rather than to splash in water.

Fig. 22.

As such a branch is not enough for many birds, I have had a little fountain arranged in the following way, says a successful breeder : a jet of water is led through five or six little holes and rises straight in such a manner that the water falls down in a fine spray and so pours on branches, placed previously in the basin, like a fine drizzling rain. In the summer green branches are used and in the winter, when these are not available, dry ones are used instead, but, if possible, covered with leaves. The basin is filled up to the edge with pebbles to prevent the birds from getting into deep water. It is really delightful to watch, when the water is turned on in the morning and pours in a fine rain on the leafy branches, fifty to sixty budgerigars in all possible attitudes trying to damp their plumage. After the bath they begin to chat and chirp with great animation, to chase each other in rapid flight, also on occasion to make love. In short, every day seems to be a festive day, since they are able to satisfy their desire to bathe. That, therefore, their state of health is excellent follows from the fact that out of about sixty specimens I bred in the course of this summer, scarcely three or four have perished.

The arrangement of a fountain for cages is shown in Fig. 23. The jet of the fountain as it is driven upwards provides the necessary humidity of the air, has a refreshing and purifying effect by laying dust, and creates in the birdroom a pleasant coolness in the summer; also, it increases the percentage of oxygen in the water which is mostly used for drinking.

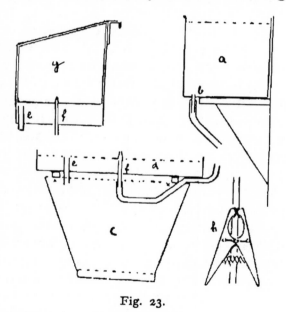

Fig. 23.

The simplest way to make a fountain for the bird-room is the following (Fig. 23): A vessel (a) is placed on a board fixed to the wall of the room. The bottom of the vessel is provided with an escape-pipe (b). A pail

(c) stands on the floor and thereon a flat vessel (d) provided with an out-flow pipe (e) and a short pipe (f) in the centre. That part of the pipe (f) which is higher than the bottom of the vessel (d) serves to receive the fountain-jet, the opening of which ought to be very fine in order that a small quantity of water only shall be used; to the lower end of the pipe (f) is fixed a tube, the other end of which fits over the pipe (b) in the vessel (a). If the distance between (a) and (d) is very great a leaden pipe is used for connecting the two vessels with a rubber-tube only at the ends. The vessel (d) is not placed right on the pail (c), but two square strips of wood are placed between in order to let the pipe through. The vessel (a) must be covered by a board in order to prevent birds meeting with accidents and to prevent the water being soiled by the droppings. Of course the whole arrangement allows of many combinations. The pail (c) can, for instance, be covered by plants or by a group of stones, etc. If the supply from (a) is to be interrupted the tube is closed by means of a clip (h).

When Budgerigars hibernate in unheated rooms or in the open the freezing of the water is prevented by the apparatus shown in Fig. 24. A cavity is dug in the earth floor of the aviary about a foot deep and eight or ten inches square, wherein a night-light is put. The opening is closed by a sheet of metal which covers the cavity, but space must be left for the air to enter. The plate is strewn with sand and the water-vessel put on it. In a birdroom with a solid floor the night-light should be placed in a wooden box, the side-walls of which are perforated in order to allow the air to enter. The lid is replaced by a metal plate.

The floor-covering should aways be dry. Wet sand must be removed immediately and replaced by dry sand. Accumulations of droppings, husks and other food residues should be removed from the cage by means of a suitable object, a little board or card. The floor-covering of the cage must be renewed at least once a week.

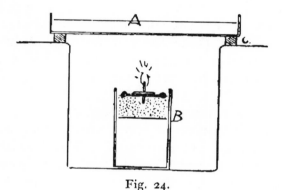

Fig. 24.

In a birdroom dirt is removed daily, the sand raked up a little and fresh sand is added. The floor-covering of the birdroom should be entirely renewed twice a year (in spring and autumn). The soil of open-air aviaries is dug or renewed once a year. Dirty nests and perches are cleaned by washing and scraping, thin twigs are cut off when dirty and replaced by new ones. A thorough cleaning of the cages must take place twice a year, likewise the cleaning of the birdrooms (in the early spring and in October).

The cages are scalded out thoroughly and scrubbed. After removing the Budgerigars from the birdroom, the whole contents of the birdroom are taken out and things still fit for use are cleaned with boiling water. Walls, floor, and so on are also washed down with boiling water. The floor is freshly-painted at least once a year and the walls newly whitewashed. After drying, the furniture is replaced.

Budgerigars must be very closely looked after. Every morning and also during the day the rooms are looked into. Husks are removed from the corn bins by blowing, dust and gravel by means of a sieve, droppings are taken out and the seed vessels filled. Water vessels and those for soft food must be kept quite clean. After feeding the birds, have a good look round to make sure that everything is in order.

When there are young ones about cages and bird-rooms may be lighted up on short winter days in order that the birds may take more food. The light should be so placed that its rays may fall on the food-vessels in such a way that the birds' shadows do not darken them. A light with a reflector is often used.

Unrest in the cages during the night may be caused by mice, a sudden beam of light, unusual noises, or the addition of a new couple where breeding is already going on. The restless behaviour of the newcomers in their unfamiliar surroundings may cause this nocturnal unrest. The causes of the trouble must be removed. Mostly Budgerigars quieten down very soon, particularly if the rooms are illuminated for some time.

The regulation of the food supply is one of the most important measures necessary to keep the birds in good health. The condition of Budgerigars kept in cages has to be checked monthly (not during brooding time). In the case of those kept in birdrooms it should be done twice a year on the occasion of the general cleaning of the room. Grasping the bird firmly, it should be turned on its back and held in the left hand in such a way that its neck is held lightly between the thumb and forefinger. (Beware of being bitten by Budgerigars. Their bite is rather painful and often the bill can be loosened from the hand it has caught by force only.) The Budgerigar held in this way lies quietly and cannot be hurt. Then the plumage on its breast and belly is blown apart and it is ascertained whether the bird is too fat or too thin. In the former case it is reduced by giving it less food, more fresh vegetables and putting it into a larger cage, in the second case it is given more abundant and more nourishing food.

Moulting does not occur at a fixed time. Usually it is finished in the course of a few weeks and it is hardly perceptible. Interrupted moulting or other illnesses to which other birds are exposed during the change of feathers rarely happens with Budgerigars. From unfavourable influences, however, the Budgerigar has to be protected as much as possible, in particular when moulting.

KEEPING DOWN VERMIN

The bird-mite, a tiny egg-shaped insect, broad and flat behind, at first white, then brown-red, hides during the day mostly in fissures and cracks of the cages, perches, etc., but also in the feathers of the bird. During the night it becomes active and attacks the birds and sucks their blood. The best preventives are cleanliness, and well-constructed cages without cracks and fissures. The use of grease, spread over the cracks and rents of the cage, and over the ends of the perches, as is usually done, causes soiling and has to be repeated constantly. Preferable is the use of good insect-powder applied in the following manner : All parts of the bird which it cannot reach with its bill are daubed with glycerine diluted with water. The bird is then powdered with insecticide by means of a sprayer. Care must be taken that the powder does not enter the nostrils, the throat and the eyes. This method, however, is seldom thoroughly successful. Spreading strongly-smelling stuffs over the neck in order to drive away the mites is useless and dangerous for the bird. The best means of fighting the mites on a bird's body is to bathe it in soapy water. This is only to be applied in case of healthy birds, not moulting or weak ones. It is carried out on very warm days in the summer. In winter the temperature should be at least 80° F., as close as possible to the stove. A lukewarm soap-solution of moderate strength is made in a dish, and in another one warmer clean water is held ready. The Budgerigar is held over the first dish and plenty of soapy water poured on it. Its head is turned upwards so that no soap suds will get into the nose bill and eyes. Then the bird is rinsed thoroughly with clean water, and so the soap is removed from the plumage. Drying is effected by softly rubbing down the plumage with soft hot towels in the direction of the feathers. Wrapped in such towels, the bird is put into a small cage and brought near the stove. After about half an hour the bird is dry. During the whole procedure it has to be protected carefully from draught, etc. Instead of the soap-solution a warm lysoform-bath (1, 5 lysoform : 100 water) can be used.

The mites in the cages are best destroyed by scalding the cage thoroughly with hot and soapy water. Cages, the exterior of which would suffer from scalding, are daubed well with a 2 per cent. solution of lysoform, then rinsed with clear water and dried. Strongly-smelling stuffs are often used, such as spirits, creolin, lysol, carbolic acid, benzene and turpentine ; the smell, however, which sticks to the cages, is disagreeable to the inmates.

Very essential for the welfare of the young still in the nesting-box is this fight against vermin, the increase of which extraordinarily weakens and even kills the young. The birds, when about ten weeks old, are carefully taken out of the nesting-box, saw-dust and other contents are thrown away, the box is thoroughly powdered with insecticide, filled again with saw-dust, or fibre of peat, and the young ones are carefully re-placed in the nest. The stand for the cage must also be cleaned.

The same methods of cleaning are applied in the case of birdrooms and aviaries. Here the best thing is a new coat of paint. To expel·mites from the nest of brooding Budgerigars is scarcely possible. Pre-ventive measures against the spread of mites should be taken always, but in particular when breeding is attempted. The spread of mites may endanger every effort at breeding. Feather mites and other parasites residing on the bird are combated in the same way.

Mice which have found their way into cages and

birdrooms may frustrate every attempt at breeding. If there are mice care must be taken that they cannot soil the food, and efforts should be made to catch them by placing traps under small cages which stand on the ground in such a way that Budgerigars cannot get near the traps.

THEIR BREEDING AND MANAGEMENT.

Budgerigars have become so popular in this country, as well as on the Continent, that a thorough treatise on their management will probably be acceptable to the many hundreds who now keep these deservedly favourite birds. Their popularity is no doubt due not only to their lovely colours and markings, but to their readiness to nest and rear a numerous progeny in confinement, either in cage or aviary.

They are now bred in a number of colour varieties including yellows, blues, cobalts, whites, olive-greens, apple-greens and jade-greens. A "Silver-wing" variety has also been produced.

These birds have been known by many names in the past, such as Zebra Parrakeet, Undulated Parrakeet, Warbling Grass Parrakeet, etc. The Budgerigar seems to be the name that is now most popular. This is evidently a corruption of "Betcherrygah," the name the Australian Aborigines call them, meaning "Pretty Bird"; the Colonists, I believe, mostly call them "Canary Parrots."

They are found chiefly on the large grassy plains of Australia, feeding on the flowers and seeds of the long grasses. Their breeding places are chiefly in the southern parts, but if it is a dry season and their food is scarce they emigrate northwards, breeding in holes in decayed tree trunks, into which they burrow like rats, hundreds of pairs sometimes nesting in the same tree.

Budgerigars average from 7 inches to $7\frac{1}{2}$ inches long; some birds, but few, measuring 8 inches. All the underparts and rump are bright grass green; the back, up to the crown of the head, greenish-black, each feather being edged with bright yellow. The flight feathers are more olive green on the outer edges, the third up to the eighth or ninth feathers having a white bar on them about half-way up, which does not show on the closed wings. The forehead and throat are bright yellow. A patch of turquoise blue appears on each cheek, with a black spot at the bottom of it, and four other black spots form a necklace round the throat. The two central tail feathers are blue; the others are dark green at the base and tip, but the central part of the feathers is brilliant yellow.

THE SEXES AND HOW TO DISTINGUISH THEM.

The sexes are distinguishable chiefly by the cere at the base of the upper mandible, which in the male is always dark indigo blue after it is about four months old. In the female the colour of the cere varies very much, but is never dark blue. In the young of both sexes the cere is flesh colour, with a bluish tinge ; the young cock gets darker blue, but the hen turns buffish.

When not in breeding condition, many hens turn quite blue on the cere ; still never dark blue like the cock. I once had a hen which reared three nests of fine young ones, but her cere remained light blue the whole of the season. But as a rule the hen's cere turns from buff to brown when breeding, and will form quite a brown scale on the cere which peels off at the end of the season, often leaving the " nose " quite blue, but not dark blue.

I should like readers to bear this in mind, that the cere of a cock bird is always dark blue and never light blue, and a hen may as often be light blue as brown, but is never dark blue. This has caused a lot of confusion in the past (as I daresay some of the large importers and dealers have found), owing to some writers merely stating that the cere of the cock was blue and the hen brown.

SOME CURIOUS TRAITS.

Budgerigars will often live to a good old age. I knew of two cocks which lived together in a Canary's " hang-up " cage for 22 years. These were some of the importation of 1879. Over 50,000 pairs were imported into England during the first six months of that year, when they were sold at a guinea a dozen. But they were nearly all cocks ; I had several dozen and there was not a hen amongst them.

These birds seldom drink in their wild state, getting sufficient moisture from the unripe grass seeds, and no doubt sipping the dew off the grass. People used to keep them without water, but I am glad to say this fad has completely died out. Still, it is an undoubted fact that they will live without water for a friend and schoolmate of mine brought several home from Australia a few years ago, and when he was leaving this country again for Australia asked me to have them. When I was bringing them away from his house, he told me not to give them any water. I told him I certainly should, as all mine drank. He assured me that they had not tasted a drop of water since he left Australia with them eighteen months before.

Mr. Wiener states that "cage-bred Undulated Parrakeets never acquire the bright green of their imported parents, and are found to breed less freely." I cannot tell whether Mr. Wiener wrote this from hearsay or experience. If the latter, it is altogether contrary to my experience, and I have bred Budgerigars now for 25 years. Many years my season's young have numbered over five hundred, and my experience is that aviary-bred birds are much larger and quite equal in colour to imported birds, and also breed much more freely.

When it is borne in mind that their natural breeding season corresponds to our winter, it stands to reason they must be in this country at least twelve months before any breeding results can be expected. Besides, newly-imported Budgerigars are always very wild, banging themselves about the cage or aviary at the slightest movement of anyone near, making themselves quite a nuisance, in fact, to people inclined to be a bit nervous. I should certainly advise anyone intending to take up with this interesting hobby to leave the imported birds to those with large outdoor aviaries, and go in for tamer, aviary-bred birds.

NESTS AND BREEDING.

If cage breeding is intended, the larger the cage the better ; I should say not less than 3ft. long, 2ft. high and 12 ins. deep. This would accommodate two pairs, for which four nests would be required. The best kind of nest for Budgerigars is the husk which the cocoa-nut comes out of. It is made by cutting a hole in the upper part of the pointed end and securely wiring the whole together, at the same time fixing some wires in the husk with which to hang it in place. It should be hung almost horizontally, the hole end a little elevated. In my aviaries I have tried every imaginable way of wiring, and with the hole at every part of the husks, and I found the birds discarded all except the ones with the hole at the end.

We will now suppose you have your cage and four husk nests. Hang the nests two at each end, close to the top of the cage, with a roost running about an inch from the front of the husk. It would be best in this case to put each pair in a small cage by themselves for a fortnight, to get paired, before turning them into the breeding cage. It may save squabbles, although these birds seldom fight, except over the husks. When two hens take a fancy to the same husk, they will fight like demons, and in the spring-time I have frequently to go into my aviaries and separate hens on the floor, for they will fasten on to each other and then drop to the ground, and there fight it out like two cats, both often being covered with blood before the battle is over.

The hens lay from four to six white eggs (some-times as many as eight or nine, but usually about six), which are laid on alternate days. The hen fre-quently commences to sit with the first egg, conse-quently there is a matter of ten or twelve days' differ-ence in the ages of the young. But the hen is careful to look after the feeding of the last-born, and it is rarely anything goes wrong with it. They sit about twenty days, but I think in very hot weather the eggs hatch out a day or two earlier.

Mr. Gedney says in his book : " The young do not leave their nesting-place until fully fledged, which stage they attain when about fourteen days old, and at the expiration of another week they discard their parents and scratch for themselves." A writer in a Fancy journal a few years ago made the same state-ment, evidently copied from Gedney's book, as any breeder of Budgerigars knows perfectly well that young Budgerigars at fourteen days old are quite help-less, and almost naked, and are not feathered fit to leave the nest until they are at least five weeks old. I make a rule of leaving the family with the parent birds until the young ones' tails are full length, and, unless for hand-rearing, it is not safe to separate them from their parents before.

HOW TO FEED.

Canary and white millet seeds are the chief articles of diet, although the birds will relish a few white oats or a spray of millet. All kinds of things have been recommended for them when they have young, but I have proved they will rear good strong young on dry seeds alone. A mixture consisting of two parts canary seed, one part Indian millet, and one part white millet will be found satisfactory. The packet seeds offered by firms of repute such as those advertising in this book can also be relied on.

As I have said, the Budgerigar in its wild state lives mainly on the ripening seeds of grasses and will generally consume green food eagerly in captivity. A regular supply of seeding grass, groundsel, chickweed and similar food should be provided. See that the grass is seeding and not merely in flower. The latter has little food value. Take care that no frosted greenstuff is offered.

When the young leave the nest, a little scalded Canary seed should be given. This is better than letting them be confined to the hard seed. The seed should have boiling water poured over it at night, and be strained through a cloth in the morning, after it has been in soak all night. This must not remain in the aviary or cage long enough to get sour.

When putting up your birds for breeding, do not forget to provide them with plenty of cuttlefish bone, also give plenty of coarse, gritty sand. To those who have the opportunity, breeding these birds in an outside aviary is far better than cage breeding, although a lady I knew bred thirteen young Budgerigars from one pair of old ones in one season in an open wire cage, about 3 feet by 2 feet, containing also Java Sparrows, Waxbills, Saffron Finches, and others.

FITS AND EGG BINDING.

I will now jot down as they occur to my mind a few things likely to crop up at times in a breeder's experience. First of all, Budgerigars are very liable to drop dead in a fit, in the Spring more than at any other time of the year; I think this must be through being deprived of green food so much throughout the Winter. Anyway, I find it a very good plan as the Winter is passing over to give, if green food is short, a little Epsom Salts in the drinking water occasionally. This must be given in a glass or china (not metal) vessel, and in just sufficient quantity to make the water taste of it.

Sometimes the bird will recover from the fit, leaving it paralysed in one or both feet. When this is so, Budgerigars will sometimes recover, but in most cases they have another attack and then "take their ticket." When a bird is found to be paralysed, the only thing to be done is to put it into a small box cage with some scalded seed on the bottom, and give in a very shallow vessel some water with a little liquid magnesia in it, letting the bird remain perfectly quiet.

Another thing the breeder will be sure to be troubled with if he puts his birds up outdoors too early—which a few warm sunny days in March are sure to tempt him to do—is having egg-bound hens. To prevent this as much as is possible, give a plentiful supply of cuttlefish, and do not pair up your birds until April. When it does occur, some hens die in the nest, and there is no help for this, as you cannot search all the husks daily. Most hens, when eggbound, however, will be on the floor of the aviary, and must be taken out at once, or the cock is sure to worry them.

After taking her out, get your little oil-can belonging to your bicycle and just dip it into hot water to warm the contents. Then take the hen in the left hand, tail between the thumb and forefinger, head held securely with the little finger. And don't forget that an egg-bound hen Budgerigar can bite; if you forget she will probably remind you of it. The back of the bird should be towards your palm. Then push the tail back with your left thumb, insert just the tip of your tiny oil-can into the vent, and squeeze it sufficiently to force out just a few drops of the warm oil. Be careful not to overdo it. Then put the hen in a small box travelling cage with seed and water on the bottom, and keep her in a warm place.

This treatment will often relieve her, although she may not lay for a day or two. But if she seems very far gone, don't wait for more than a few hours after the oiling, but hold her vent over a small jug of hot water, trying the latter with the back of your hand first, to see that it is not too hot. After she has been steamed, if she does not soon lay, I hold her in my hand as before, and place the thumb and forefinger of the right hand on each side of her vent, and very gently press. She will at once feel the help, and though apparently so far gone as to be insensible, will at once begin to strain to relieve herself of the egg. After two or three " strains " you will see the white egg appear, as just a little white spot.

You must have a friend or helper with you then, possessed of a steady hand, and a small needle. Both your hands, of course, are occupied, and if you leave off the pressure of the thumb and finger the hen will stop straining and the egg will go back. Get your helper to prick the egg with the blunt, or eye end, of the needle, being careful to prick nothing but the egg. This will let out the contents, and the shell will collapse and come away without further trouble. A hen which has been through this process should be kept by herself for a week. Continental breeders recommend pure cod liver oil mixed with the canary seed fed to the birds—two teaspoonsful to $3\frac{1}{2}$ pints of seed—as a preventive of egg-binding.

DEFICIENCIES OF PLUMAGE.

Very often after the second round of nests, it will be found that young ones are leaving the nests without their long flight or tail feathers, but with the whole of the body and head perfectly feathered. This I believe to be caused not by in-breeding, as some say, but rather by over-breeding—that is, when the parent birds are beginning to get exhausted. I never discard these young ones, for the father of my Lutino

Budgerigars, pure yellow with pink eyes, which I once bred, never had any long flight feathers for years, although his progeny were always perfectly feathered.

The best thing to do with these misfeathered youngsters is to put them into a large cage, wired only in the front, with the roof low down. Keep plenty of sawdust on the bottom to prevent them injuring the end joint of their wings when trying to fly, and as the moulting season comes on, buy some sulphate of iron. Instead of putting a little lump in the water, as is often recommended, put it in a clean, old jug, and pour some boiling water over it and stir up. When cold, pour off the solution into a bottle for use. A few drops of this in the drinking water (just sufficient to tinge it) well stirred up, is far better than putting a lump in the birds' water and leaving it to dissolve after the birds have drunk.

It will be found that most birds minus tails and flights will come all right at the moult under this treatment. Or Squire's chemical food may be used for the same purpose, but this is much more expensive.

It is often the case that before one nest of young are out of the husk the hen has commenced laying again ; consequently the eggs get very much fouled by the excrément from the young. In this case you will need a teaspoon, a small hog's-hair brush or bit of flannel, and a basin of hot water—not too hot, but so that you can comfortably bear your hand in it. With the spoon take the eggs out of the nest and put them in the water, taking care they do not roll out of the spoon. After soaking a few minutes in the water, the dirt will easily wipe off with the wet brush or bit of flannel. Let them dry and return them to the husk.

CURIOUS HISTORY OF THE LUTINOS.

Speaking of hot water reminds me of a curious thing which happened regarding my pair of pink-eyed Lutino Budgerigars, and which made me think I had discovered a way of producing Lutinos. But whether my action had anything to do with it I must leave scientists to say. Looking round the husks to see that all was going on right, I noticed in this particular husk—which was near the ground, as the cock could not fly well—three eggs, two of which were quite covered with excrement from the last nest of young. As I knew the hen had commenced to sit, I called to my wife to bring me out a basin of hot water and a spoon, which she passed into the aviary to me. I put the spoon into the husk and brought out the two eggs, which I dropped into the water.

My wife's attention for the moment was taken up with some other inmates of the aviary. She then happened to look round, and, seeing what I had done, instantly exclaimed : " Charlie, you will kill those eggs. The water was boiling when I brought it out." I whipped them out of the water at once, wiped them clean, and put them back into the nest, though never dreaming they would hatch. But they did. And, strange as it seems, those two eggs produced what I believe to be the only Lutino Budgerigars ever known !

I kept these birds for two years and both bred with greens, but try as I would I could not get them to breed together. They were purchased by Miss Howison for something like ten pounds, at the Cheltenham Show, where they won me the cup for the best exhibit. When the late Mr. Joseph Abrahams afterwards saw them exhibited by Miss Howison at a show in London, he told me he would gladly have given me twenty pounds for the pair had he known they were Lutinos.

I am afraid to say how many eggs I have since spoilt in experiments, but without producing any more Lutinos. I should like to know if the water being too hot was likely to have influenced the colour of the young.

RED MITES, CANNIBALS, AND CATS.

Breeders will sometimes find the husks get infested with red mite. In this case get some Pyrethrum powder, and with the small bellows sold to use with it, blow plenty of the powder into the nest. It will not hurt the young, only make them cough until the dust settles. But transfer them to a new husk as soon as possible, which, remember, must be hung in the same place.

Sometimes a hen turns out a perfect cannibal, first biting the skin, and stripping the skull-bone of her young ones bare ; if not seen in time, indeed she will then chew them to rags. The culprit can always be identified, as she does not wash the evidence of her guilt from her face, which will be covered with blood. I think my remedy for this sort of thing is the best and quickest. I catch the offender, take her outside the aviary, where the ground is covered with large flagstones, and, lifting my hand as high as I can reach, I dash her to the stones with all my force. This is quicker than chloroform.

I have seen fanciers recommend, when birds (and animals as well) have any unpleasant trick, to " get rid of them.'' I think that means simply passing your own trouble on to someone else, which no straightforward fancier should dream of doing. I may add that if one of these cannibals be allowed to remain in the aviary after tasting blood, she will soon recommence operations on other young after her own are gone.

Anyone breeding Budgerigars out of doors must be careful to guard against cats. When I erected my first lot of aviaries I used only galvanised netting of half-inch mesh, thinking this would secure the birds against any cat. But as soon as the young began to leave the nests my troubles began.

For the first week or so after the young are out and about, their favourite roosting method at night seems to be to hang with the hook of the upper mandible to the wire netting, holding on as well with their feet. The cats see them, climb stealthily up the netting, catch hold of a foot with their teeth and pull until the leg comes away from the body. The bird seldom dies as one would think, but the blood and feathers dry over the wound, and the first thing you notice is that you seem to possess birds which must have been hatched with one leg, for after a few days there is not the slightest sign of their having ever had two.

The remedy for this state of things is double wire. The outside wire should be at least two inches away from the other, and ¾in. mesh will do well for it, besides being not so dear.

BREEDING BUDGERIGARS WILD.

It has often been suggested that Budgerigars would do well wild in this country, seeing that they stand our winters so well out of doors. This has been tried, but proved a complete failure owing to their migratory instincts. The birds migrate from one part of the Australian Continent to the other, according to the grass season.

Some years ago, Captain Spicer, of Spye Park, who is a great lover of nature and birds especially, consulted me as to stocking his park with them. I thought it was a grand idea ; that we should be able soon to claim the Budgerigar as a naturalised British bird. I supplied the captain with sixty pairs, all large, strong, aviary-bred birds, and with over a hundred wired husks, some of which were hung in a wired enclosure, and others about the house and park. As there is a large deer park round the house and several very watchful keepers, there was little fear of the birds getting shot or destroyed.

The sixty pairs were put into an open wire place where they had room to exercise their wings and have a good look round at their surroundings. After about a fortnight a small door in the netting was let down, and they were allowed to go in and out at will, a good supply of seed being always kept in the aviary ready for them. They soon made themselves at home. Some nested in the old decayed trees about the park, but the majority seemed to prefer the husk nests that were provided for them.

All went on swimmingly, and when the first nest of young were out they appeared to be everywhere. Every one who heard of the experiment was delighted. But alas! "The schemes of mice and men gang aft agley." When the Autumn came, although food in abundance was provided for them, all except about twelve pairs disappeared never to return. Those that remained the Winter through did well, and commenced breeding early in the following Spring. I had a young one, about seven weeks old, brought to be stuffed, which had been killed at the end of March about seven miles from Spye Park; so its parents must have nested successfully in mid-Winter.

All the birds seemed to do well and breed freely that Summer, but in the Autumn every bird disappeared this time, and I have not heard of a single specimen having been seen on the estate since. So if anyone else contemplates repeating the experiment he must be prepared to renew the stock every Springtime.

SOME CONCLUDING HINTS.

Young Budgerigars do not get their yellow forehead until the first moult. Until then the pencilling on the head is continued from the crown down over the forehead. They get their yellow forehead when about six months old, and the sex can generally be told then.

Care must be taken to guard against in-breeding, or the stock will soon degenerate, and instead of being larger and better birds than imported specimens, they will come small, weakly and featherless, some being not much larger than a Siskin. Here is the best plan to adopt, supposing you have breeding room for fifty pairs :—

The importation of Budgerigars usually takes place in the Spring. If some good birds arrive from Australia, get 25 pairs of them. But be careful to examine their feet and claws to see that none are missing ; also, be sure to keep them in quarantine for a few weeks to see that they are free from septic fever. Many of the Australian Parrakeets, Rosellas and Pennants especially, die off wholesale from this disease after arriving here (as I know to my cost), caused by overcrowding, dirty cages and foul water during the voyage.

When you have your 25 pairs of Australians, pick out all the cocks and put them with 25 of your own aviary-bred hens. Then put the Australian hens with your 25 aviary-bred cocks. These will breed you young which you should be proud of ; quite as good in colour as imported birds and much larger in size.

The yellow or mealy Budgerigars are no doubt produced chiefly by in-breeding ; consequently they are not so hardy as the green ones. The late Mr. Abrahams told me he thought the yellows could be produced from greens in seven generations, but I think they are got from yellows cropping up now and again among the young. I have had them crop up two or three in a season, before I had any yellow birds in my aviaries.

Breeders should be careful not to have an odd, unmated hen in the aviary, as she will cause no end of mischief, turning out eggs, killing young ones, and quarrelling with the other hens. But an unmated cock or two seldom works any mischief in this respect.

Mr. Wiener says : " Talent for learning to talk the bird has none, but one or two authentic cases are recorded of Budgerigars learning to say a word or two, probably about as well as the talking seal (called talking fish) once exhibited in London." Now in spite of what Mr. Wiener says, I can assure readers that Budgerigars hand-reared from the nest have wonderful talent for learning to talk. I have had and sold some really fine talkers, as I have letters to prove. They quickly realised five pounds each, so, of course, they are not quite so plentiful as blackberries in Autumn. I have one now—about nine months old, a very distinct talker—more so than many Amazon Parrots. He says : " Joey's a beauty," " Dear Joey," " Kiss pretty Joey," " Oh, you beauty," " Open the door, please," " Let Joey out," etc. There is no need to tell a listener what he is saying, as is often the case with Parrots.

Budgerigars must be hand-reared to become thoroughly tame, as they cannot be tamed by giving them tit-bits, like many other birds, for they refuse anything but seed. To hand-rear Budgerigars is a rather tedious task, as the seed must be scalded, soaked, and then shelled before giving it to the young birds, which should be taken from their parents when the tail is about an inch and a half long. Thev can then be accustomed to being carried about on the hand or head, and will fly from cage to finger, etc. Anyone who has a tame, hand-reared talking Budgerigar has one of the most delightful pets imaginable.

Should anything have been overlooked in this section on these favourite birds of mine that readers would like to know, a letter to " Cage Birds " will receive prompt attention and advice.

BREEDING

ABOUT the size of small breeding-cages all that is necessary has been said in Chapter V. In view of many unfavourable experiences Dr. Bilfinger considered it necessary to breed Budgerigars only at the rate of two couples in a cage measuring three feet each way. Under these circumstances it is much easier to carry out the necessary cleaning of the cages, to watch the course of brooding and to become acquainted with the peculiarities of each of the hens. Larger houses intended exclusively for breeding Budgerigars, and in which many couples are to be kept must be constructed on different lines than those followed when breeding a few in a small cage. An average of about 30 cubic feet per couple is necessary, so that in a two-window room of an average size of 15 × 15 × 9 feet about fifty to sixty couples can be accommodated. Breeding on such a large scale, however, would probably turn out a failure, because it would be impossible properly to look after so many.

NESTING ACCOMMODATION

As to nesting accommodation Budgerigars are not hard to please. In several cases they have managed without, hatching the eggs on the floor of the cage and rearing the young without difficulty. This happened even though nesting boxes were ready. For every couple two nesting boxes must be available. They are made in many different shapes. A good nesting box for Budgerigars should be about 10 ins. high and 6 ins. wide, with the entrance about 1¾ ins. in diameter, and cut 6 ins. above the floor. (See Figs. 25-30).

The best shape for a nesting box is cylindrical (a hollowed-out log answers well) ; square, hexagonal, or octagonal nest boxes, made of boards ½ in. to 1 in. thick are equally useful ; those which are made of bark

Figs. 25, 26, 27, 28.

are less suitable. The inner floor should be hollowed out into the shape of a saucer so that the eggs cannot roll apart. The roof should be flat and projecting over the box in front and at the sides. The walls of the nesting boxes, especially the inner walls, should be rough or grooved parallel to the bottom. The top of the nesting box should be made to open.

Perches at the entrance are not required. Birds nesting in holes do not find these necessary.

The inner bottom is covered with a thick layer of sawdust or peat-fibre.

MATING

Like all other parrots Budgerigars mate for life. Their love is so ardent that they are not outdone in tenderness by the parrots known as Love-birds, a tenderness which has become proverbial. " Their mating," says Dr. Bolle, " reminds one in its fervour of the classic myth of Leda and the swan. The hen

Figs. 29 & 30.

bending back her head towards the cock which takes hold of her bill with his own and embraces her with his long wings." As in the small cage, so in the large aviary one always finds the couples together. They live, however, in a very remarkable relation, for matrimonial quarrels, which happen not infrequently with all other parrots, even with Love-birds, never occur with Budgerigars. The cock follows the hen everywhere, caressing and flirting; during brooding it feeds it out of its crop and nourishes the hen and the young ones almost completely till the latter have entirely grown up. In very exceptional cases a strong old cock in the birdroom consorts with two or three hens, each one in a special nesting box. But even then he attends particularly to the legitimate wife and her offspring, while looking after the others only occasionally. It also happens that two hens peacefully brood together with one cock and bring up the young ones jointly. Seldom has a female been observed to pair with two males.

Breeding-birds must be chosen carefully. They should be healthy, as big as possible, strong, well-fed and not be blood-relations. The plumage should be well developed, vividly coloured, smooth, and without bald spots. Defective plumage is usually a sign of degeneration; the cere of the bill should be smooth and shining, a wrinkled cere is a sign of old age, degeneration or illness; the bill should not show any defect; the legs should be strong, not bent or knock-kneed, the toes and claws undamaged; movements should be energetic, the whole bearing sprightly and alert. Male and female should be as nearly as possible the same size, though slight differences in size are insignificant. Where there is a difference it is better that the female should be the bigger.

AGE OF BREEDING-BIRDS

Young Budgerigars sometimes nest at an astonishingly early age, but they should not be allowed to brood until they are at least one year old. Nesting earlier, they are naturally only able to produce weak offspring in which at birth or when growing up the foundations of degeneration are laid. If on the contrary it is asked how long the nesting-age lasts—for similarly birds that are too old can only produce weak and degenerated offspring—no exact statement can be yet made. Parrots in general reach a comparatively great age, but it is most probable that this proportion will differ in the case of the smaller varieties. Hitherto, however, it has been observed that Budgerigars properly treated reach the age of twenty years and more, and judging by this the full breeding powers are likely to last five to six years at least. The maximum fertility of Budgerigars is reached towards the end of the second and in the beginning of the third year.

The mating-up of breeding couples has to be effected in special cases, discussed below, by the breeder himself by keeping the birds to be mated for a week or fortnight separate in a cage. As far as possible the couples should be allowed to mate when by themselves.

All birds should be put into the breeding-room at the same time. Although the feuds of couples put in later are of short duration much harm can be done by putting in others after breeding has started.

On principle one should see to it that the couples are complete. Surplus cocks may be present in the breeding-room, as they do not cause any disturbance, but join zealously in feeding the young which are flying out, but are not yet full-fledged. Unpaired females will start quarrelling and fighting, which often results in a sanguinary murderous set-to. Any real furies which attack other females had better be removed. The method of splitting with a sharp-pointed knife the large wing-feathers of one wing of those dangerous hens has been applied successfully. Thus they are prevented from flying swiftly and are unable to pursue the others.

The marking of breeding couples and of the young, particularly when breeding coloured Budgerigars, is absolutely necessary for systematic breeding. Breeding of coloured varieties must not rely upon products of chance. The relationship of every bird to be used for the purpose of breeding must be exactly known in order that even slight changes of colour can be strengthened or suppressed by a corresponding supply of suitable blood. Therefore a permanent and thorough marking of the young is strictly necessary. That is also required in order to be able to distinguish the old breeding couples from the fully-developed young ones and to carry out line-breeding and eliminate the dangers of in-breeding.

Marking by colouring of the under-surface of a wing, by clipping a large wing-feather, or by incisions in the feather is not expedient, because the mark is difficult to recognise, disappears in the moult and has to be renewed.

In order to mark Budgerigars efficiently leg rings of celluloid or metal are used.

Closed leg-rings to be fixed on the young ones in the nest are useless because of the thickness of the ball of the foot. Besides, the adult birds would try to remove the rings from the feet of their young and possibly injure them.

Numbered aluminium rings, as used in the " Breeding-station, Rositten," are, according to the experiences of Mr. Schwarzkopf of Ingelfingen, unsuitable, because even young birds destroy these soft rings easily with their bills. But Dr. Wagner, of Warmbrunn, has had very good results with aluminium rings. His Budgerigars have worn the rings for about four years and no bird has yet removed them. The unfortunate experiences of other breeders have been attributed by Dr. Wagner to the quality of the aluminium of these rings. Dr. Wagner had good results with rings of zinc-wire. By the use of gilded zinc-rings many variations can be obtained which make it possible to distinguish the birds even at some distance. If one group is fitted with a zinc-ring on the right foot, another with the same on the left foot, a third with two right, a fourth with two left, the fifth with two right, one left, the sixth with a zinc-ring and a gilded one on the right, etc.

Rings of brass and German silver are used by another breeder. By providing the left or right foot with rings, different combinations are possible. The young birds of the first brood are provided with plain rings, for the birds of the second brood the rings are notched with a file. Spiral celluloid-rings make strong, permanent identification marks and are best for Budgerigars. These can be obtained in about eight or ten shades. The colours are so vivid that the birds thus marked can be distinguished at a distance, and there is no need to catch them.

Overlapping flat celluloid rings are simple strong rings of a diameter of about ⅛th in. They can be easily put on and removed.

Celluloid-rings closed by means of acetone are used successfully by Mr. Grasl of Vienna. The method is as follows : The bird is held in the left hand, head downwards, thumb and forefinger stretching the foot which is to be ringed. With the right hand the open ring is placed on the foot, both ends of the ring daubed with acetone by means of a brush, and then pressed tightly upon each other by means of flat pincers and kept thus for about half a minute. The acetone dissolves the celluloid and evaporates very quickly so that the dissolved mass becomes hard. The ring can then only be removed from the foot by severing it with nippers.

Care must be exercised in this process as acetone is highly inflammable. After pressing with the flat pincers the ring should not fit so closely that the leg is pinched. Otherwise swelling of the foot and sores would result. Then the narcotic effects of acetone must be borne in mind. This liquid evaporates very quickly and its effects are similar to those of chloroform. It is therefore better to provide the birds with rings in the open, though the risk of any misadventure is not great. Once a young female Budgerigar while being rung received a few drops of acetone on its feathers and afterwards reeled about for a time on its perch as though intoxicated. In any case the acetone bottle should remain corked as much as possible, especially when the process of putting on the rings is carried out in an enclosed space.

The rings for Budgerigars can be easily made at home. Celluloid factories supply cheap coloured plates of the strength of cardboard which, when soaked in hot water, can be cut up into strips with a pair of scissors. These strips can, while still soft, be bent round a nail or a slender stick and will keep their circular shape when dry.

It is safest to put on the rings before the Budgerigars

leave the nest or immediately afterwards. At this age the birds are still too helpless to free themselves from these shackles and later, when they have got used to them, they make no attempt to do so.

Mr. Schwarzkoff says : " In an outdoor aviary the use of celluloid rings is insufficient. This year I am keeping in my aviary about twenty Budgerigars—olive and yellow as well as green of different shades obtained by colour-breeding—flying about in perfect freedom. So I have no alternative but to ring the young ones before flying and after ascertaining the parents, which are all provided with rings. The rings are numbered consecutively, for I am expecting more than a hundred young ones and I want to trace the descent and colouring through several generations, which means that I am going to establish their pedigrees. For that purpose an indestructible and unlosable ring properly numbered is absolutely necessary. I have got a sample ring from the maker and I am going to try it this year. This is a closed, strong, numbered, aluminium ring inscribed with the date and breeder's mark. It remains to be ascertained what age is the most suitable for putting the rings on the young birds so that they cannot be stripped off, but can be fixed on without forcing and hurting the feet. As several females were already hatching I had to decide, and I resolved to make the experiment mentioned."

The nesting time of Budgerigars bred in Europe lasts throughout the year. The Australian Budgerigars during their first years in Europe observe the nesting time of their native country, December, January and February. They nest at this time with extraordinary eagerness and good results.

The hen lays one egg every second day. Old and very strong hens lay one egg every day. The average number of eggs in a clutch is five. When brooding for the first time the number is smaller, about three. Clutches of eight and, in rare cases, of twelve eggs have occurred.

Incubation lasts sixteen to eighteen days, according to the temperature of the room. In most cases the hen sits alone, fed and carefully watched by the cock. Sometimes the cock will brood at the same time with the hen or alternately. In the former case they cover the eggs between them, sitting in contrary directions. When one of them leaves the nest the other spreads itself as much as possible in order to keep the whole clutch warm.

Some people have observed that Budgerigars turn the eggs several times an hour. Baron von Freyberg maintains that it is done three times an hour.

The young are blind, and at first entirely nude and ugly creatures, but after some days they are covered with a thin yellowish-white down and from about the sixth day they show the first signs of feathers. Now the down grows darker, to a whitish-grey, and as soon as the yellow tips of the wing- and tail-feathers are showing, the blue spots in front of the neck appear. On the twelfth day they open their eyes and grow comparatively quickly, so that they are able to leave the nest after thirty to thirty-five days. The tip of the bill develops slowly and is perfected only a short time before flying. The statement, however, that the bill only then becomes curved and that three toes at first point forward is incorrect. These develop from the beginning in their natural form. When leaving the nest they have their nestling plumage which commences to change colour from six to eight weeks after flying. First the forehead becomes lighter. According to development the change of colour is effected in six to nine months, and then the young bird is ready to breed. Sometimes, as already mentioned, the desire to mate develops earlier, before the change of colour is entirely completed.

REARING THE YOUNG

Immediately after leaving the shell the young begin to chirp and the more they grow and put on flesh the louder and livelier become their voices.

The feeding of the young ones in the nest is carried out, as is probably the case with all young parrots, in a remarkable way. O. Strassberger relates in *Monatsschrift des Deutschen Vereins zum Schutze der Vogelwelt*, 1896 (p. 47 and 48) that often, when inspecting the nests, he found the young Budgerigars lying on their backs and that they are fed in this attitude. The young parrot in the first days of its life is incapable of lifting up its comparatively big head. K. Lotze reports in *Gef. Welt*, 1901, p. 60 *et seq.*, as to the breeding of Grey-parrots : " The young bird is seized with the curved hook of the upper bill and put on its back ; thus its bill is turned upwards and the food can be administered. After being fed, the young one is turned again by means of the crook-bill." Probably the feeding of young Budgerigars in the first days of their life is done in the same way. The time between the laying of the first egg and the day on which the young ones leave the nest is on an average 8 weeks, but the hen starts sitting immediately after laying the first egg. So the young are not hatched all at the same time, but one by one, and in the same nest one finds almost fledged birds by the side of unfledged ones. Sometimes the hen even lays the eggs of another brood before the young of the first have flown out, and these help in hatching the second lot by their own warmth. During the brooding period till just before the young become fledged the hen stays in the nest, only leaving it for some minutes a day to ease herself and to shake up her plumage. She then slips into the nest again mostly without touching the food. She scarcely takes time even to drink. She is fed exclusively by the cock and herself feeds the young birds. Later on the cock joins her in feeding the young and a long time after their flying out, when the hen is still sitting on the younger ones or has started hatching anew, he still feeds those that have flown. The couple then develop astonishing activity, the cock time and again fills its crop with seeds, etc., empties the contents into the bills of the hen and the young and repeats this untiringly early and late. It is an admirable trait in the hen that in the winter nights when she has to stay in the nest for fifteen to seventeen hours, seemingly without receiving any food, she is yet able to keep the young alive and bring them up. It has been ascertained by close observation that Budgerigars even during the night feed the young. About every half hour or every hour the chirping of the young has been heard and the hen has been noticed to come up to the opening now and then and receive food out of the crop of the cock which is sitting on a perch before the opening. If the male meets with an accident the female mostly brings up the young all alone. Attempts have been made to accustom

Budgerigars to feeding by artificial light in order that from dusk till late in the evening they should still be able to take food to the females and young. Illuminating of breeding-rooms is, however, not strictly necessary as Budgerigars can feed in the dark as mentioned above.

The hen, at least in most cases, keeps the nest scrupulously clean by throwing out the dirt of the young with its bill. If, however, the nesting-case is too narrow, or the hen does not remove the droppings, vermin appear in large quantities, and not only mites or bird-lice, but also fleas. In this case the half-grown young, which suffer considerably from parasites, are lifted carefully out of the nest and put into a second which has been carefully cleaned. This nest is fixed in the spot where the first had hung before. When lifting the young beware of breaking the quills which contain blood, for thereby the plumage will be mutilated for a long time. Brooding Budgerigars are mostly indifferent to disturbances by the intervention of their owner, particularly when the young are already hatched. So it has happened in cases of removal that nest-boxes in which hens were hatching or rearing young were subjected to long journeys, and then hung in a birdroom new to them ; or that a nesting-case which had hung in a birdroom was placed in a cage. All this did not prevent the birds from hatching out the eggs or bringing up the young. The male was conveyed in a special box.

From large clutches, it has been observed, not more than six young have as a rule been brought up, the last hatched dying some days after coming out of the shell.   In order to save these last Mr. Grasl (*Gef. Welt*, 1923), suggests the following method : " . . . in these cases I sort the young in the nests according to size. I often observed that nine or ten birds living at the same time in one nest prospered well and all of them became fledged provided that the difference in their ages was not more than eight to ten days.   Out of a clutch of eleven eggs, for instance, I left six young birds with the parents, while those that were hatched later were immediately afterwards put under another couple which had only yielded unfertile eggs.   All five step-children became promptly fledged."

REGULATION OF BREEDING

The couples should not be allowed to nest too many times in succession.   For the sake of the profit or from thoughtlessness it has happened that breeding was allowed for years on the same scale.   In that way the old birds are weakened too much, so that the hens best fitted for breeding die, weak and sickly young are produced and the first cause of degeneration is created. In order to prevent ceaseless nesting, it has been suggested that the sexes should be temporarily separated. Such a method, however, is not advisable because the hens, when shut up together, often attack and kill each other and sometimes they continue laying eggs in spite of the absence of the cocks, and so are weakened just the same.   The method of leaving the sexes together, but removing the nesting-accommodation, is not of much use, because they then lay their eggs on the floor.   The only safe way is to catch all the birds in a large breeding-room after six to eight months' diligent nesting—that is, after three or at most four broods. Each should be examined and put by itself in a small cage and fed according to its condition with meagre or nourishing food. After six or eight weeks they can be put into the thoroughly cleaned and newly arranged birdroom again.

Breeding Difficulties

With all parrots it sometimes happens that a clutch of eggs or a brood of young suddenly disappears. Inspection of the nest shows a clutch of a certain number of eggs, next the chirping of the young can be heard, but at the next inspection no trace can be found of either the eggs or young. Among the litter of the nesting-box, however, one can trace a half-eaten egg, a small bone or a wing. In most cases the hen herself has destroyed the brood in that way. Sometimes also she ill-treats the young when they leave the nest not yet quite fledged, plucks them till they are bare, or even kills them. Such cruelty is caused by a morbid impulse ; the bird must be removed quickly out of the breeding-room ; it should be paired with another strong male and the couple afterwards bred in a cage of their own.

Even tried hens frequently, after one brood has flown and the next is started, become cruel and aggressive. As it is not advisable to catch these birds Dr. Bilfinger, an experienced breeder of Budgerigars, soothed them successfully by sprinkling thoroughly with lukewarm water every hen that tried to attack others or to slip into occupied nests. Then they would search for their old nests or for unoccupied ones. If nothing is done to prevent this behaviour, broods, particularly those with already half-grown young, are greatly endangered as hen Budgerigars are only inclined to keep off intruders when they are laying eggs or sitting on them, or when they still have very small young.

Similar statements are made by Mr. Grasl (*Gef. Welt*, 1923) : " I wish to draw particular attention to another circumstance which often frustrates the breeding of Budgerigars—I mean the destructiveness of some hens. These furies, according to my experience, are of much more frequent occurrence than most people think. There are birds which have been the best mothers for a long time, but suddenly they decide to move into another nesting-box. The young inside are simply killed, and the couple occupying the desired nest is expelled. If the endangered brood can be placed under other couples in time, the expelled couple, after a few days, become resigned to another nest and start brooding there again without being further disturbed. But there are still more dangerous hens which are not content with driving away only one family. I mean those which wander from nest to nest, scaring every pair and killing all young. Such birds are mostly bad rearers themselves and frustrate every effort at breeding. Even in a cage of their own, they are of little use as a rule, and should be disposed of."

Sometimes it happens that a couple of Budgerigars are unwilling to start nesting, although all conditions are favourable and all possible preparations for successful breeding are made. Mr. Grasl calls attention to a circumstance which generally brings about the desire to breed, and which is little known. This is, to excite mutual jealousy among the birds. It is therefore a good thing when attempts at breeding are made to place two or more couples in the breeding-cage together.

Another hindrance to successful breeding lies in allowing the young to nest too soon. Young birds have been observed to start nesting at five or even three months. Such birds, especially when originating from the same nest or from the same parents, often show themselves permanently or for a very long time unfit for breeding either because of exhaustion or for other reasons. There is nothing for it but to separate this couple and pair them with fresh, strong, imported birds. But of course the separated couples must not be left in the same room, or there will be no nesting at all.

HAND REARING

Should Budgerigars desert their unfledged young, it may be necessary, if the brood is a valuable one, to feed by hand. This is also necessary if one wishes to train them to repeat words, etc. The following advice is given by Mr. W. v. Lucanus in *Gef. Welt*, 1925 : " Hand-rearing is not too difficult, but takes a lot of time. The birds should be taken out of the nest-box when they are half-fledged but still entirely incapable of flying. At that age the body and particularly the structure of the bones is already so far perfect that artificial rearing does no harm as a rule, and the foster-children do well. Losses of course are unavoidable. They have to be faced from the first. But if the young Budgerigars are reared carefully, not too many of them will be lost. If the birds are nearly fledged then it is mostly very difficult to accustom them to the artificial manner of feeding which I am going to describe. They already know their parents, the inborn shyness of men is already developed and it is hard to persuade them to accept the rearing-food. The first Budgerigar I reared was entirely feathered when I took it out of the nest. Not till the third day, when it was quite weak and exhausted, did it resolve at last to take the offered food. It did well, became very tame and learnt to speak excellently.

" If the birds are taken out of the nest when still very young and in their down, they get used to hand-rearing without any difficulty, but on the other hand there is the drawback that they easily die. The artificial food lacks a very important ingredient, that is the mucous secretion from the crop of old birds, which seemingly plays an important part in the nourishment of the young. It apparently contains ingredients which are very important for the formation of the frame and cannot be replaced by such artificial preparations as salt and lime. At least I had no success with these in the case of young birds. A good substitute is in my experience powdered charcoal which, in very small quantities, is added to the rearing-food.

" The great value of the mucous secretion of the crop of old birds for the nourishment of young granivores is clearly proved by the fact that pigeons feed their young for the first few days exclusively on the mucous secretion of their crop, the so-called pigeons'-milk. Anyone who has large parrots can secure the mucous secretion of the crop for rearing small parrots in the following way. Grey-parrots, Amazons and Araras frequently, under the stimulus of sexual excitement, eject the contents of their crop in the presence of the keeper. They wish to caress their master in the usual way of parrots and feed him out of their crop. An affectionate parrot is easily stimulated by caressing. I then catch in a spoon the contents of the crop which are thrown out in large quantity, and mix it with the rearing-food. Thus I have obtained excellent results.

"The artificial rearing-food is prepared in the following way : a thick gruel is boiled of shelled millet and wheat groats to which a little ground charcoal is added. The millet has previously been crushed to a fine meal in a mortar. I usually take one-third of millet and two-thirds of wheat groats when preparing the food, but it can also be mixed in equal portions. In order to make the food a little varied I use maize meal on some days instead of millet or wheat.

" The gruel is offered fairly warm to the birds in a small spoon, say a tea-spoon. It should still steam a little, but must not be too hot. As the contents of the crop which are administered to the young birds by the old ones are warm, rearing-food also must be heated. The young birds immediately refuse to accept the food if it is cooled down. The reflex action of swallowing is induced by heat.

"The old birds, as is well known, feed by seizing the bill of the young with their own and then emptying the seeds soaked in their crop into the throat of the young. Young parrots do not open their bills in order to be fed like young starlings and other birds. Therefore rearing is more difficult. At first it is necessary to accustom the bird to eating its food from a spoon if one doesn't wish to feed it out of one's mouth, which is not to everybody's taste. It is not advisable either, as too many bacteria are transferred to the bird by human saliva, which may have undesirable consequences. Parrots are greatly subject to tuberculosis, which is easily transferred by men, as everybody has tubercle-bacilli in his saliva without necessarily being ill himself. The bird, after having been taken out of the nest, is at first left without food for 24 hours, which does no harm. Then the owner takes it with one hand, dips its bill into the warm gruel and moves the spoon gently to and fro. Thus the bird gets the sensation of being fed by its parents. It is very hungry and in most cases will swallow part of its food immediately. If it does not at once it generally will decide to do so after one has repeated the movement several times. Then the owner has gained his point. In a short time the birds get accustomed to artificial rearing. As soon as they see the spoon they lift themselves up in their nest, flutter their wings, beg for food and eat eagerly out of the offered spoon. But one should take care that the food really is warm enough. As soon as it cools down a little during feeding the birds cease to eat. Then it must be heated again. One should have a little spirit-stove ever ready for that purpose. After the meal, the remaining food should be kept in a cool place. The gruel easily turns sour, therefore it should be made freshly each time. It must not be boiled too long, for that diminishes the nutritive value of the food.

" As soon as the young are fledged, they are kept for several days in the artificial nesting-place before they are allowed to fly out. They then possess more power of resistance and do not so easily meet with accidents.

After 'they have flown out, some millet and canary seeds are strewn on the floor of the cage in order to accustom the birds to eat unaided. It is not necessary to soak the seeds. On the contrary, the young birds prefer hard seeds to soaked ones. The bill of a young, fledged bird is already strong enough to shell seeds. To coax the young to eat alone is the most difficult point in rearing. Time and again they beg the keeper for food and cannot make up their minds to feed themselves. In the wild state the young are fed by their parents for a long time after they are fledged, and it is this habit which makes rearing so very difficult. A King-parrot had to be fed by me after being fledged for almost two months. It ate by itself to some extent, but not sufficiently to be properly nourished, and begged for food time and again when seeing me. The best way to break the obstinacy of the bird is to give it into the care of other people. The entirely changed circumstances, especially the absence of its master whom the bird knows very well, then force it to be independent. After a few days the bird is accustomed to feed unaided and can be taken back again by its owner. In freedom young parrots are probably forced to be independent simply through being left by their parents, who start nesting again. The success of rearing in general depends mainly on arranging all things as naturally as possible.

" Thus one obtains charmingly tame and affectionate birds. I had very tame Budgerigars which I had reared myself and other parrots which came and sat on my hand directly when I called them and followed me everywhere. The birds learn to talk and to whistle tunes if they are at all inclined that way. In this respect I had most success with some Budgerigars about which I wrote in *Gef. Welt* on a previous occasion. My cock Budgerigar ' Puck ' developed into a first-class talker. He spoke many sentences and phrases, counted correctly up to ten and sang the verse, ' There is a little blue flower, its name is forget-me-not,' besides imitating many other things. Cocks are much better pupils than hens. The same is the case with the Nymph-parrot. I brought up four young Nymph-parrots, but unfortunately all were hens which never learned anything."

TREATMENT WHEN FLEDGED

The young Budgerigars are generally good-humoured and peaceful. The whole lot fly about cheerfully in the birdroom and with their pastimes—climbing, teasing each other and chirping ceaselessly—they do not usually disturb the nesting couples. If there is room and they are all well taken care of, it is advisable to allow the young to fly about till breeding is over, as they frequently join in feeding those young which have just left the nest, in the same way as the surplus old males do.

Sometimes, however, the young Budgerigars, as soon as the brooding instinct awakes in them, which often happens very early at the age of three months, slip into nest-boxes and destroy eggs and young ones. Therefore many breeders, in spite of the advantages of leaving the youngsters in the breeding-room, think it better to remove them as soon as they are entirely independent. The young ones are then accommodated in large flight cages and for some time continue to get the food they had in the breeding-room. When caught out of the birdroom and locked up in cages they are very excitable, especially if roused by any noise during the night, and are liable to injure themselves.

In-Breeding and its Results

WHEN breeding is conducted on a very large scale various drawbacks manifest themselves. Degeneration sets in and with it weakening of the body and various kinds of diseases. The same phenomenon, as is well known, is observed in the breeding of all other domestic animals if this is not carried out rationally. Dr. Neubert, of Stuttgart, Baron von Freyberg, of Nürnberg, and several later breeders have made remarkable statements about degeneracy caused by continuous reckless in-breeding. The result is lasting weakness and demoralisation, so that by the third generation the birds have practically lost their reproductive powers, and in the fourth generation, if it is possible to obtain such, they are quite incapable of doing so, and can scarcely live. Therefore one never should continue breeding beyond the third generation without importing fresh blood. Young couples for breeding should be made up from self-bred ones paired with freshly imported ones or with birds obtained from other breeders. In order to breed economically it is not enough to choose carefully Budgerigars of one's own breeding or those purchased, but one should breed a special stock for this purpose. The newly-imported birds are often exposed to several maladies and even epidemic diseases, and therefore they may be used for breeding only when they have recovered and are quite acclimatised. Self-bred Budgerigars very soon show signs of degeneration and therefore one has every reason to choose only the strongest and healthiest specimens. If for the purpose of breeding on a large scale one mates imported cocks with self-bred hens and then, after two years, crosses their young with imported birds and repeats the same process every two or three years, one obtains a breeding-stock which will certainly be healthy and strong. Two separate breeding-rooms are required for that purpose, it is true, in which the sexes are brought together alternately, or it can be managed by way of exchange with another big stock-farm, so that every year cocks and hens are exchanged while fresh blood is continually procured. Newly-imported couples are bought every year and alternately each stock-farm takes one year all the cocks and the next year all the hens.

The first sign of degeneration is always leg weakness. The limbs are unnaturally turned aside so that such a Budgerigar is from the first unable to stand erect, but according to the degree of its degeneration appears straddle-legged, staggering and awkward, and in the worst case it even grows up lying flat on its belly, unable to use the weak legs at all. In other cases the weakness is noticeable in the wings, so that the birds are unable to fly or only fly clumsily, while the rest of their body seems to be healthy. Still others have defective plumage and appear to be moulting permanently all their life, so that some parts of their body always remain bald. Young ones have been bred lately on a large scale which lack the large wing-feathers and the long tail-feathers. Further, in the case of birds weakened by degeneration, the young which should be ready to slip out of the egg, are often found dead in the shell because they are too weak to break through. Finally, incipient degeneration has also influenced the colour. The measures to be taken to avoid such degeneration are simply to avoid carefully going against nature; secondly, breeders must tell each other their experiences, follow those attentively and act accordingly; and, lastly, in their mutual dealings honour and sincerity must be always observed.

It happens frequently that a breeder who follows carefully all the advice given above and who looks well after his Budgerigars, will yet breed scrofulous, degenerated birds. Each such couple must be separated and mated with others. If the hen or the cock in the new couple still produces cripples, the same method is applied again; if, however, this measure also fails, the bird is no use for breeding and must be destroyed. All weaklings, sickly and featherless or otherwise degenerated birds, but particularly the crippled young, should always be destroyed at once. Only on condition that this principle is practised strictly, can the breeding of Budgerigars retain its vitality. As long as the young grow bigger and stronger than their parents, their plumage more beautiful, more glossy, more richly and gaily coloured, their body built more strongly and their fertility increased—our breeding is on the right lines. The Budgerigar is closely connected with the canary in regard to its adoption as a domestic bird. Like the canary, it is exposed to unfavourable and favourable influences and its breeding requires the utmost precaution. Young birds which are still immature, or only artificially and unnaturally mature, weaklings and sickly birds can, as said before, only produce poor off-spring exposed to various kinds of degeneration and in the third or fourth generation the course of breeding ends miserably. Besides, even quite healthy and strong young Budgerigars sometimes leave the nest imperfectly feathered, when hatched in an overheated room or when suffering from vermin.

BREEDING RECORDS

When breeding in cages, the breeding of two couples in a cage 3 ft. 6 in. long has yielded the best results.

I will quote a few statements about the productiveness of breeding Budgerigars in former times, as they show how prolific these birds are under certain circumstances.

"My three newly imported couples," says the chemist Schuster, of Rössel, "had in July twenty-four eggs altogether, seven, eight, and even nine in one nest, from which eighteen young Budgerigars were hatched and left the nest in August. As early as the 13th of September there were again twenty eggs in the same nest. All the young are very pretty and strong birds." In the house of Mr. Friedrich Geissler, of Langenburg, two couples in one year reared eighty-six young, with from four to seven in each brood. In my own birdroom eighteen young in two nests became fledged the same day. The maximum number of one brood is said to be twelve. The highest total, however, is probably that recorded by Mr. W. Elsner, of Berlin. He obtained in about two years from two couples 118 young birds without losing a single hen through laying difficulties.

Extraordinarily good results have been obtained in aviaries and it is to be hoped that this way of breeding will attract more attention. Mr. Grasl in the summer of 1922 obtained from six couples kept in two aviaries the following produce :

Couple I, 2 Broods, 32 Eggs, 18 young fledged.
,, II, 3 ,, 17 ,, 15 ,,
,, III, 2 ,, 16 ,, 0 ,,
,, IV, 4 ,, 25 ,, 20 ,,
,, V, 3 ,, 24 ,, 18 ,,
,, VI, 3 ,, 24 ,, 9 ,,

That is in all eighty young reared from 138 eggs. In addition it should be mentioned that seven young ones were killed by older birds, six met with fatal accidents, and eleven died from lack of proper food.

ATTEMPTS AT ACCLIMATISATION

Budgerigars that have escaped have not only been known to live in freedom, but have even bred. On the estate of a Belgian count two couples escaped in the spring which were not recaptured and were considered lost. There was no little astonishment when in the autumn a whole flight of them appeared and were seen feeding in an oat-field. It was discovered later that they had been nesting in the holes of the stems of willows and increasing from seven to twelve or fourteen. A Dutch farmer shot a Budgerigar which seemed to be well fed in spite of the fact that it probably had been free for a long time. Other cases of the same kind have occurred. Luigi Althammer tells of a couple which escaped in the Tyrol in April of 1862, and not only nested in the open, but even flourished during the next winter. Many lovers of Budgerigars recently attempted to acclimatise them in suitable places where large old trees or pollard willows grow near fertile corn-fields, meadows, kitchen-gardens, etc. Hitherto no details about the results have been communicated, but I have no doubt that the Budgerigar would get used to our climate. But there is one obstacle which makes it almost an impossibility, and that is the fact that every strange bird of striking appearance is always shot down at once by sportsmen in the woods and fields.*

* The strong migratory instincts of Budgerigars defeated an attempt to acclimatise them in England on a considerable scale. Sixty pairs were allowed their liberty in a deer-park surrounding their aviary. Breeding went on extensively during the summer, but when autumn came, although food was provided in plenty, all but a dozen pairs disappeared. These bred freely during the following spring and summer, but with the approach of winter every bird vanished.—ED.

Colour Varieties

In some countries, particularly Belgium and France, the breeding of various coloured Budgerigars, especially the blue variety, is highly developed and of late also in Germany and Austria, many fanciers are turning to the breeding of coloured specimens. In the bird periodicals of France, Belgium and England coloured Budgerigars, mostly blue ones, are regularly offered for sale. At the great bird shows a wide range of coloured varieties are displayed.

All animals which have become domesticated and bred in captivity for many years are inclined to change their colour. In the case of birds there is, as with domestic poultry, the tendency to become white, called albinism, that is, the disappearance of any pigment from the plumage, and in the case of the canary and also of the Budgerigar, there exists the tendency to become yellow, which is only a first step towards albinism.

The absence of pigment in the plumage is a symptom of degeneration which must not be connected with degeneration of the whole organism.

But considering that all coloured Budgerigars, no matter of what hue, are with only a few exceptions more delicate and frail than the natural birds, and are generally also smaller and weaker; and furthermore, that their offspring is less numerous, and that imperfect development of some organs is not rare, it is clear that we have to deal with a symptom of degeneration.

The symptoms of degeneration seem to increase the more, as the colouring of the variety differs from the colouring of the natural bird. So we still find among the naturally-coloured " blue blood " Budgerigars strong birds, which sometimes even surpass the natural bird in size. The smallest and most weakly ones are the sky-blue Budgerigars—probably also the very rare white ones—the size of which is mostly a third smaller than the size of the normal bird.

Besides the symptoms of degeneration mentioned above, there is still another externally perceptible one, especially in the case of the blue variety, the imperfection of the wings which also appears in natural birds degenerated by in-breeding. The wings are, in many cases, incompletely feathered. These stunted birds, it is unnecessary to say, are unsuitable for breeding. Unfortunately they are bought and sold as "young sky-blue Budgerigars."

There are other symptoms of degeneration. " The females often suffer from laying difficulties, the eggs are often smaller than those of the green birds, the number of sterile eggs in a clutch is comparatively larger and rearing of the young is not always easy. Particularly strongly-built young ones in the nest which surpass their brothers and sisters in size to the satisfaction of the breeder, turn out eventually to be green throw-backs when the feathers are grown."

" Further, the bad habits of hens in destroying clutches and broods of others, scarcely observed in the case of imported birds and in isolated cases only among ordinary Budgerigars bred in Europe, seems to be the rule in the case of highly-bred coloured varieties " (Stefani in *Jahrbuch* 1925 der A.Z.).

The dangers of degeneration must be counteracted by the breeder in every direction. This is done by following the advice given about the choice of birds for breeding. Then he must provide for coloured Budgerigars as favourable conditions as possible. This consists in keeping each couple apart in very wide cages which allow as much freedom of movement as possible. Stefani affirms that a minimum length of 3 ft. 6 in. per cage for one couple is necessary and this cage must be placed on a balcony or verandah or in any case in the open during the warm season. Better still is a garden aviary or something like it, at least 6 ft. long. When the birds hibernate in the open, which can be done when the aviary is placed in a sheltered situation or can be protected by such measures as windows, etc., the area should be still larger.

Mr. Richard Schwarzkopf, of Ingelfingen, says in *Gef. Welt*, 1924: " To notice the first signs of degeneration in the broods requires a sharp eye and thorough knowledge in the breeder. It is possible to avoid difficulties by letting nature have its own way as much as possible. Man is not able to recognise the morphological qualities of the live animal and the physiological qualities only after long observation. Therefore free selection is to my mind the method which will lead in the quickest and most certain way to the end in view. For nature alone carries out the complementary measures necessary for preservation of the races in pairing the individuals. The yellow variety of the

Budgerigar is according to authorities without any doubt a product of in-breeding, if it is not already a symptom of degeneration. Therefore this variety is frail and delicate. It is different with the blues. At least I have hibernated so-called "blue-blood" Budgerigars—sky-blue beneath and partially blue up to the crop—in an open-air aviary, and in spite of cold and snow I brought up several broods. In the spring there is great activity, up to six young ones have flown out of one nest and the percentage of birds of blue extraction is high. In order to supply fresh blood I am willing to effect exchanges with owners of blue Budgerigars . . . but I certainly believe that it will be possible to produce blue Budgerigars in this way also in Germany." It will scarcely be possible, however, always to allow "free selection" as probably most of the breeders do not possess material for breeding in such abundance that they are able to apply free selection. Besides it appears doubtful whether this free selection would really produce the effects Mr. Schwarzkopf assumes.

But attention may be drawn to his reference to the supply of fresh blood and a union of all breeders of coloured Budgerigars with common interests in order to render the supply of fresh blood possible. Renewal of blood, that is crossing with unrelated individuals of another strain may have good results as regards size, vitality and fertility. In-breeding, that is the pairing of parents with their own offspring, or pairing of brothers and sisters, preserves the peculiarity of the coloured variety, but leads to more or less rapid degeneration which can be prevented by the supply of fresh blood.

In order to obtain the desired success a breeder of coloured Budgerigars must know the laws of heredity. Mr. Schwarzkopf (in another publication) says quite rightly that he who claims to be a breeder to-day ought to be familiar with the Mendelian laws of heredity, whether he breeds animals or cultivates plants. If he does not know them, his pairing is only playing instead of breeding and the products of his cross-breeding are only products of chance which may be very valuable in the hands of the experienced breeder, but are useless for breeding purposes in the hands of the layman. If one wishes to reach one's aim there is required in addition to insight, the gift of observation and knowledge, as well as plenty of room and appliances for breeding. To find out whether an animal is surely homozygote or heterozygote requires individual treatment and many periods of breeding. Two animals are necessary for breeding and it may take a long time to ascertain which one is homozygote or heterozygote, and it can be very expensive too, unless the breeder is so lucky as to pair two homogeneous animals by chance. The dangers of in-breeding are added to those difficulties. A new line of breeding, in our case the colour of Budgerigars, cannot be reached without sensible in-breeding. Here the physique and the organic functions of the parent animals play the decisive part.

It is Mendel's great merit to have recognised that the hereditary tendencies of the parents do not amalgamate into entirely new ones different from those of the parents, but are preserved side by side.

Mendel made experiments chiefly with plants. But

it has been shown that the rules found for plants apply equally to the heredity of animals.

In the diagram given on p. 113 illustrating Mendel's laws of heredity we can see that in the first generation the characteristic of one parent, the red colour, is dominant (d.) over the characteristic of the other parent, the colourless white and the latter, though present, is recessive (r.) Mostly the original form will be dominant over the results of breeding. So when crossing naturally-coloured Budgerigars with coloured varieties the native colour will be dominant over the derived colour of the domestic state, which means that all young birds will be coloured naturally.

The descendants of this first generation will also show the natural colour dominant and that in the proportion of three to one. Thus three of the young birds would be naturally coloured and one only would show the colour of the derived domestic form.

But neither are the three naturally-coloured birds homogeneous. Only one would transmit the pure natural colour. In the two others the colour of the variety is present, but is recessive, and if these two were crossed the descendants (third generation) would be graduated again in the following proportion : one naturally coloured bird, two mixed (with the natural colour dominant and the colour of the variety recessive) and one bird having the colour of the variety. There are thus three quite different forms present in the proportion 1 : 2 : 1, two of which, however, only appear in the proportion 3 : 1. The birds which in these two generations already have their colour unmixed are called homozygote.

The birds which have one colour of their parents

dominant and the other one recessive, that is present, but not appearing, are heterozygote.

Both are of value to the breeder. The homozygotes are purely coloured birds of pure heredity when in-bred ; the heterozygotes are used for breeding homo-zygotes, that is birds which transmit the pure colour. This is achieved by interbreeding heterozygotes with the result 1 : 2 : 1 or by crossing homozygotes with heterozygotes. The result is shown in the diagram.

This kind of heredity which is characterised by the dominance of either one or the other characteristic mark of the parents is called alternative heredity.

About another kind of heredity which does not show dominant and recessive characteristics, Dr. Braune says in a paper, " Colour-breeding of Budgerigars," published in *Gef. Welt*, 1923 : " Further investigations have shown that dominant and recessive characteristics appear by no means always in cross-breeding. If one interbreeds, for instance, the red-blossoming with the white-blossoming Marvel of Peru (Mirabilis jalapa) the blossom of the first cross-generation is without excep-tion pink. These pink flowers, however, have pink as well as white and red offspring and that in the same proportion as the peas : one red and one white, both with purely coloured offspring, and two with pink blossoms which in their turn split up in exactly the same way. In this case, therefore, the pure specimens can be at once distinguished by their exterior from the cross-specimens, as the latter represent a com-promise. From the exterior of the pink variety one would think that it is a real mixture of both colours, but the reappearance of the original red or white blossoms, as the case may be, in the following genera-

he law of Mendel in crossing red-and white-blossoming Peas (alternative heredity).

▦ = red-blossoming pea = $\frac{red}{red}$

◻ = white-blossoming pea = $\frac{white}{white}$

$\frac{red}{red} \times \frac{white}{white}$

First Generation.

All individuals are red. Formula $\frac{red\ (d.)}{white\ (r.)}$

Red is purely and absolutely dominant (d.)
White is recessive (r.) i.e. latently present but does not appear.

Second Generation.

$^1/_4$ of the individuals are red ($^1/_4$ unmixed, $^2/_4$ mixed) $^1/_4$ white.

Interbreeding of $\frac{red}{white} \times \frac{red}{white}$ thus produces the following $^1/_4$ $\frac{red}{red}$, red unmixed; $^1/_4$ $\frac{red}{white}$, red mixed; $^1/_4$ $\frac{white}{red}$, red mixed; $^1/_4$ $\frac{white}{white}$, unmixed white.

$\frac{red\ (d.)}{white\ (r.)} \times \frac{red\ (d.)}{white\ (r.)}$

$^1/_4$ $\frac{red}{red}$ $^1/_4$ $\frac{red\ (d.)}{white\ (r.)}$ $^1/_4$ $\frac{white\ (r.)}{red\ (d.)}$ $^1/_4$ $\frac{white}{white}$

Third Generation.

$\frac{red}{red} \times \frac{red}{red}$

$^1/_4$ $\frac{red}{red}$ red unmixed $^1/_4$ $\frac{red\ (d.)}{white\ (r.)}$ red mixed $^1/_4$ $\frac{white\ (r.)}{red\ (d.)}$ red mixed $^1/_4$ $\frac{white}{white}$ white unmixed

when close-bred constantly red

$\frac{red}{white} \times \frac{red}{white}$

$^1/_4$ $\frac{red\ (d.)}{white\ (r.)}$ red mixed $^1/_4$ $\frac{white\ (r.)}{red\ (d)}$ red mixed $^1/_4$ $\frac{white}{white}$ white un-mixed

$\frac{white}{red} \times \frac{red}{red}$

$\frac{red\ (d.)}{white\ (r.)}$ $\frac{white\ (r.)}{red\ (d.)}$

$\frac{white}{white} \times \frac{white}{white}$

when close-bred constantly white

Cross-breeding of homozygotes with hetero-zygotes.

102

tions clearly shows that in the generative cells the tendencies remained unmixed."

This kind of heredity is called "intermediary heredity."

In the paper in question Dr. Braune says further : " Now about our coloured Budgerigars. The natural primary colour is green with the well-known marks and designs in other colours. Yellow is albinism from green, so-called ' Xanthism ' as in the case of our canary, and is, according to the way in which it appears, to be considered as a pronounced mutation.*

"Absolutely yellow Budgerigars (total albinism) when paired together will always produce yellow offspring. If one obtains from yellow parents also green young, one may be sure that at least one of the parents is not ' pure,' that is, it shows only partial albinism.

* Among varieties, no matter whether in regard to colour or other characteristics, we make according to their origin two main distinctions—Variations and Mutations. The former kind presents itself as small and insignificant deviations from the characteristics of the parents. By casual—or in the case of artificial breeding, deliberately caused—coincidence of such (at first very small) variations in the parents, they can reappear in the children in a more marked degree. At last, after a series of generations, they may lead to pronounced marks deviating from the original form. So a bluish tint of the plumage can, by the pairing of two such parents, develop at last into a distinctly blue tone in the plumage of the young, which then becomes more or less constantly hereditary.

Much more quickly than variations, mutations have the same result. By mutations we mean the sudden deviations from characteristics of the parents appearing in the young ones as it were by leaps, which are often observed. To these belongs albinism characterised by a sudden appearance of white in hairs or feathers and red eyes, which points to the lack of the normal pigment in these structures.

Variations as well as mutations behave in the same way in regard to heredity, only mutations lead to the goal more quickly. Both are usually recessive in case of meeting with a normal consort. Their entire disappearance in the first generation therefore does not at all mean a failure to the breeder. The next generation will enlighten him about the real situation.

From yellows paired with absolutely green birds one may expect naturally coloured green ones ; these, however, paired together or with unmixed yellow ones, will show the characteristics of heterozygotes—that means, they will produce yellow as well as green offspring in proportion. As, with regard to these proportional figures, we have of course always to deal with chance possibilities, the exact proportion cannot be obtained by a small, but only by a long series of experiments.

" Whether the glossy satin-coloured Budgerigars (or satin-greens as they are usually termed) must be considered as variations or mutations is undecided.

" The blue Budgerigars are most likely to have arisen by variation, i.e. by gradually breeding for a more intense blue colouring.

" The olive-green ones seem, according to Freytag, to be a mixed colour of blue and green. The blue-greens seem to possess the same potentialities, only the blue perhaps in a very small degree, but in this case the two colours do not appear mixed. Further breeding will probably bring more and more exact knowledge. This applies also to the jade greens which are said to be a product of crossing blue, yellow and green. Amateurs can still do a good deal of laudable work for science in this regard.

" The reader may guess the unlimited possibilities we have ' to deal with in such breeding experiments. The breeding of coloured varieties of the Budgerigar is no simple matter, but all the greater is the interest of the breeder and the pleasure which success gives."

OLIVE-GREEN BUDGERIGARS are probably the result of systematical selection from yellow Budgerigars with an olive-green tinge. They are distinguished from the naturally coloured bird only by the pronounced olive-coloured tone of the green plumage. The olive-green is sometimes brighter, sometimes darker. Also in another way, however, have olive-green Budgerigars been produced of a very dark shade, as well as light or emerald-greens and beautiful dark greens with a bluish shade and blue under tail-coverts, and " sky-blues." The following communication from Mr. Mayer of Lucerne (*Gef. Welt*, 1924) gives the following information on this point : " In the years 1916 and 1917 many hundred couples of green Budgerigars passed through my hands intended for export to America. My critical eye soon discovered several birds among them showing a distinctly blue gloss. I thought here was a fine opportunity, carefully picked out those specimens and already imagined a flight of these beautiful blue Budgerigars. But alas! As these birds with undoubted blue blood were a bit small and weakly, and I feared crippled offspring, I made the great mistake of inter-breeding them with the big strong green Budgerigars from my own stock, and so I had to wait full five years till the blue blood was dominant again. At last in June, 1922, the memorable event happened. During an inspection of one of the nests in the room where I keep the birds for breeding I noticed two sky-blue Budgerigars and two dark olive-green ones. In the next brood were a sky-blue bird, an emerald-green one, and a dark green one. In the third brood were four birds, but all of them a nice dark-green with a bluish tinge. That was all! Once while feeding, the male of the couple was struck by apoplexy and died. Last year I replaced it by one of the dark green sons of the first brood after the mother had refused pairing with the blue son. The result was good. The first brood yielded two sky-blue birds and two dark green ones and the second brood five green ones, two of them light or emerald-green, three of them dark green. This year I have mated five couples, avoiding as much as possible too near relationship, all with strongly blue blood, while two of the females were an unmixed blue. Now I have already twenty-four young birds, strong healthy specimens, but none of them a pure sky-blue, but I still hope to get sky-blue ones. They are partly emerald-green, partly dark green, partly tending towards an olive-green hue, but all with a decided blue tinge and an almost clear blue plumage at the under-surface of the tail. It is interesting that in three places in Switzerland, where I had disposed of some of my green birds of last year and the year before, a blue one has been bred this year. It is by no means easy to breed distinctly blue ones from green Budgerigars and the inter-bred blue birds are weakly, soon degenerate and the colour fades, which means that they soon turn whitish till at last they become a clear white. Only by mixing with blue blood is that rich deep sky-blue colour obtained which is so beautiful."

The dangers of degeneration have been avoided by Mr. Mayer by " letting nature have its way as much as possible." But I do not believe that by breeding in this way alone the aim of breeders of coloured varieties will be realised.

The JADE-COLOURED BUDGERIGAR is a coloured variety of particular beauty. To produce it, naturally coloured yellow and blue Budgerigars are said to have been used. Mr. Stefani proposes in "*Jahrbuch* 1925 der A.Z.*"* to call it the May-green Budgerigar : " In the foliage of birch trees in May one would entirely overlook the bird, as it is coloured exactly like the leaves." The dark pencilling is of a grey-green colour. Mr. Freytag, of Wiesbaden, obtained by cross-breeding " jade-coloured " and " blue blood Budgerigars," green young ones with light blue abdomen.

SATIN-GREEN BUDGERIGARS are described by Mr. Lichtenstaedt as " splendidly coloured birds. The abdomen is a deep shining green beautifully resplendent in the sun, one of the prettiest parrots . . ." Young birds of this variety distinguish themselves from the naturally coloured bird by a slightly darker green. A " slightly " bluish tinge of the plumage of the under parts I have never been able to observe. Sellers saw it. The gloss is said to develop only at a greater age. They are said to be bigger and stronger than the natural birds.

As a throw-back resulting from pairing olive-green Budgerigars, Mr. Stefani in another place mentions ORANGE-COLOURED BUDGERIGARS showing a rich yolk-yellow which suggests orange-colour. For the rest this variety resembles the yellow Budgerigar. It is a deeply coloured throw-back to this variety to which probably the olive-green ones owe their existence.

BLUE-BLOODED BUDGERIGARS are, as a rule, particularly large and strong birds resembling the natural bird, which they are said to surpass in size, with the exception of the plumage of the abdomen and sometimes also the under tail-coverts, which show a more or less distinct blue tinge. They represent reactions from breeding blue birds. Paired together, the blue-blood

Budgerigars produce naturally coloured young ones which probably, like their parents, are valuable for breeding the blue variety.

BLUE BUDGERIGARS. " No bird all over the world," reports Mr. van der Snickt in 1881, " has caused so much admiration and at the same time so many expectations as the blue Budgerigar of Mr. L. of Uccle. This bird is quite free from yellow with the exception of the bill, which appears yellowish; the head is snow-white with pitch-dark design, eye-ball white, iris black ; back black, blue and ashy-grey ; breast sky-blue. This was a male bird, and was paired with a yellow female. The young ones obtained were all yellow. In the course of the summer (1881) Mr. K., also of Uccle, bred another blue Budgerigar, a female, which was blue all over its body. Head and tail, however, were yellow. Unfortunately the two blue birds were not paired ; the female is now brooding with a yellow male. I had also heard of two blue females and both were promised me. But when I arrived to fetch them, I found both lying dead on their eggs and already in such a state of decomposition that I could not stuff them.

" Now at last I have obtained the female I desired so long from the couple which, three years ago, brought forth the male. It is not yet quite perfectly coloured, but it is already plain that it will be as pretty as the older one."

The SKY-BLUE BUDGERIGARS, rather widely bred nowadays, show a nice sky-blue where the natural bird is green, and the yellow part of the plumage has turned into white. Otherwise it is just like the natural bird. The birds offered for sale as " COBALT-BLUES " show a dark blue plumage. There are also blue Budgerigars, which still show a clear yellow, particularly at the head.

The first blue Budgerigars excited the ecstasy of bird-lovers. Mr. Pracht describes in *Gef. Welt*, 1924, the impression the birds made on him: "The long cherished hope is fulfilled. Before me is an observation-cage with the precious contents—a couple of absolutely blue Budgerigars. Everybody who sees them is as enchanted as I am. All fears that the blue ones would only differ in colour from the natural bird, but that the colour would not equal the very pretty primitive bird, are extinguished. The blue Budgerigars combine the beauty of the green one with the green replaced by a marvellous sky-blue. When once the blue ones are as easy to breed as the other varieties and, therefore, become more accessible and cheaper, then the verdict may be changed, as experience teaches. Whatever appears in large quantities, though ever so pretty, soon suffers neglect. The colour of the blue Budgerigar is distributed as follows: where the primitive bird is green the blue artificially-bred bird is blue. On the tail-coverts the blue colour also has the metallic gloss of the green bird. Where the primitive bird is yellow (upper head, throat and edges of the wing-feathers, feathers of the wing-coverts, edges of the eyelids) the blue Budgerigar is a creamy white. The throat shows the clearest white. The little beard is a deep dark-blue, the dots on the throat a still deeper blue. The bill is like the primitive bird's. Differences due to sex are also the same. The feet are delicately pink and almost transparent. The claws are grey. The eyes black. Where the primitive bird has the black rippled marking the blue, the artificially-bred bird has a very delicate grey, almost dun marking. The long tail-feathers are analogous to the green bird's, but all blue. In their singing, chirping, chattering with each other, feeding each other—in short, in their general behaviour, they closely resemble the primitive bird. How could it be otherwise? They have the same body and the same instincts as the primitive birds. Breeding only gave them another pigment or withheld a part of the pigment, or mixed them otherwise, as the result of the intervention of the breeder. The product of this intervention is so charming that, as mentioned before, I am not the only enthusiastic follower. One of the Budgerigars is just shaking up its plumage and between the wing-coverts the upper back, rump and the upper feathers of the tail-coverts become visible and show their glittering blue splendours. These parts bear comparison with the shining parts of the plumage of the king-fisher.''

The experience hitherto of German breeders with the blue-coloured variety shows that without systematic breeding the producing of blue Budgerigars is merely a matter of chance. The results of breeding published below show that clearly.

Dr. Mayer, of Lucerne, obtained blue birds by cross-breeding blue-blood birds and natural birds. The result was :

First brood : Two sky-blue birds, two olive-green ones.

Second brood : One sky-blue bird, one emerald (light) green one, one dark-green one.

Third brood: Four dark-greens with a bluish tinge. One of the dark-green young ones mated with the naturally coloured mother :

First brood: Two sky-blue birds, two dark-green ones.

Second brood: Two light-green birds, three dark-green ones.

An attempt with five birds bearing a strong strain of blue-blood, among them two sky-blue females, yielded :

Twenty-four young birds of different varieties of green, no sky-blue bird.

Mr. Lichtenstaedt, of Berlin, obtained from a highly blue-blood couple with intensely light-blue under-surface :

Four young ones with a delicate green on the upper-surface which seemed as it were powdered with blue. The under-surface was intensely sky-blue. They developed into naturally coloured birds, only a little blue on the under-surface remaining.

Mr. Schwarzkopf, of Ingelfingen, bred from Budgerigars with blue blood " a good percentage of birds with blue heredity."

According to the other statements sky-blue Budgerigars are said to be produced by inter-breeding birds of blue blood with olive-coloured ones.

All this shows that these products of chance do not make us achieve the desired object.

WHITE BUDGERIGARS.—Dr. E. Rey, many years ago, observed among the birds bred by him a variety with a broad, clear, white stripe across the wings. At the same time the plumage was on the whole of a duller hue, the green was more bluish and the blue more slate-coloured.

In 1897 L. van der Snickt, of Brussels, related that breeding of yellow Budgerigars also yielded birds with partially white feathers.

" These latter do not form a constant variety, they are the same as the yellow ones with a slightly green gloss on the back and breast, the whole plumage canary-yellow, no traces of pencilling nor the dots at the throat ; the spots on the cheeks are white, and gleam like silver; the tips of the tail and the wings are white, bill and feet are flesh-coloured, eyes red, nostrils reddish. It seems peculiar that among seven birds with red eyes and white spots on the cheeks which I had occasion to observe I did not find a single male. Would that be accidental ? All the young ones of these albinos paired with green males were green ; one exception only resembled the female."

The white variety is rarely to be found. The plumage is a clear white with a fine gloss. The design which is black in the case of the natural bird is here a dim lustreless white.

Mr. Stefani mentioned in another place also MOUSE-COLOURED BUDGERIGARS, probably impurely coloured birds of the white variety.

MAUVE BUDGERIGARS mentioned by Mr. Mayer, of Lucerne, in *Gef. Welt*, 1924, have come from sky-blue birds. Their ground-colour is a bright violet-blue with a touch of pink.

DARK CREAM-COLOURED BUDGERIGARS were bred by Mr. Lichtenstaedt, of Berlin, by systematical selection from yellow birds. In perfectly coloured condition they had about the colour of young newly-fledged yellow Budgerigars.

BLACK-HEADED BUDGERIGARS have been offered for sale by a Liverpool firm. I do not know whether we have here to deal with a product of chance or a result of colour-feeding. Probably the latter. Mr. Stefani reports (in another place) that a bird lover in the Rhine provinces possessed " two green colour-fed Budgerigars, one of which has a beautifully fiery red, the other a brownish-red head, otherwise their natural plumage is quite unchanged." The endeavour to obtain coloured varieties of the Budgerigar by colour-feeding is a useless pastime for breeders of Budgerigars, as pigments would have to be administered continually in order to preserve the colours thus obtained. Unfavourable results would be sure to follow.

YELLOW BUDGERIGARS.—The first traces of flavism were discovered in the bird which was bred by Dr. Rey and described above, a Budgerigar with a white stripe across the wings. This cross-stripe gradually turned yellow. An almost canary-yellow Budgerigar was bred by Mr. Stechmann, director of the zoological garden of Breslau, with the following markings : the young bird showed upper-surface dim and pale, greyish-green-yellow, edge of forehead intensely yellow, with indistinct dark cross stripes ; upper head, sides of the head and neck, pale grey-green cross stripes ; nape and upper back pale-grey with bright yellow spots. Central and lower back and rump a clear glittering grass-green; primaries feebly yellowish-white, exterior vane more intensely yellowish, tip dark-grey, secondaries more vividly yellow with broad grey tips, the first wing-feathers on the under-surface almost clear white, the rest yellow-white, all with grey tips ; feathers of the first wing-coverts bright yellow with grey tips ; all other feathers of upper wing-coverts irregularly grey with yellow spots, the small under wing-coverts yellow-green, the large ones yellow, on the right wing grey ; upper tail-coverts greenish-yellow ; tail feathers yellow, the two central ones pale yellow, the others more vivid, all with bluish-green tips and dark ribs, on the under-surface likewise bright yellow, all with grey tips ; beard vividly yellow, the blue spots small and delicate, vague on the left side only, the blackish spots small and delicate ; neck and throat bright yellow ; breast and belly yellowish-green ; sides and thighs a clearer green ; central part of the belly, hind-quarters and under tail-coverts blue-green ; bill horny grey-white ; feet grey-white. Size at least a third smaller than the natural bird. In the birdroom of Mr. Stechmann there was also an extremely pretty and strong male, the two central tail-feathers of which appeared bright yellow instead of blue.

" I do not doubt," thus Mr. L. van der Snickt wrote me in 1878, " that the Budgerigar, like the canary, will produce different races and varieties in a comparatively short time. For more than ten years past Mr. Kessels in Uccle (Holland), one of our most important lovers and breeders, has possessed extremely large and strong Budgerigars, bred by him in such a way that every time he saw a female which was a little larger than usual he bought it and put it into his breeding-cage. Last winter about ten of his Budgerigars were stolen, and when, somewhat later, strikingly large Budgerigars came on the market, he immediately recognised his own and was able to give up the thieves to the police. The first yellow Budgerigars I saw as early as 1872 were in possession of Mr. T. Boone, among 150 naturally coloured couples. I wished to buy them, but they were not for sale. Then I advised keeping the yellow ones apart, together with the adult which reared them ; however, they all perished accidentally. The second case was a yellow couple in a flight of more than 200 couples in Brussels ; this was sold to a lady for 500 francs, after which yellow young ones came out of the same nesting box again. In the summer of 1877 I counted in a small aviary, among fifty couples, fourteen yellow birds ; not all were, however, a clear yellow, some of them were greenish at the belly and back. Through the intervention of a dealer we brought fifty young ones out of the same cage the next autumn in order to continue breeding in a special room. Unfortunately, they all died shortly afterwards. In the zoological garden of Antwerp, there is also a similar variety but not a clear yellow." Later on (in 1878) the same author writes : " In this year more success has been obtained with yellow Budgerigars. One can divide them into the real yellow variety and albinos (mentioned above). Recently, however, I discovered in an aviary an entirely yellow female with here and there a dark green feather at the breast and almost black stripes on the wings. At a public sale in Antwerp there were also six yellow Budgerigars. These young birds were a dirty greenish-yellow with pale grey undulations and did not look pretty. Four of them have been bought by Mr. Westerman, director of the Zoological Garden of Amsterdam. The rest are in my possession. Another variety seems to be quite yellow at first sight, but when looking closely one notices a slight greenish gloss and on the neck and back traces of greenish-grey undulations ; beard-spots slightly blue, tips of the wings and of the tail white. Another variety is brimstone-coloured all over the body with very pale grey undulations on the neck and back ; the black spots of the throat are grey, spot on the cheek pale blue, feet flesh coloured, eyes black ; the male has a blue cere. From one couple Mr. Kessels bred in two broods at first one, then three young birds. Mme. Bodinus, who obtained a couple from me, has also bred twice, each time five young ones. All these young birds resemble their parents, only they are more regularly yellow.

" Only twice I saw yellow Budgerigars with black marks. One is stuffed, the second is the property of Mr. K. This gentleman has specialised in breeding canary-coloured Budgerigars without any undulations and with red eyes. In the spring he wanted to bet that he would obtain twenty-five a year. He succeeded, but, as I warned him beforehand, all twenty-five turned out to be females. Although 150 francs apiece have been offered him he will part with none of them. He hopes that it will be possible eventually to breed pure yellow males without undulations and with red eyes."

Mr. Hauth, of Potsdam, in 1881, obtained from a couple of yellow Budgerigars at first a dark yellow male. The ripple, however, was still visible. A second brood yielded seven young out of ten eggs, five of which became fledged ; three males were again a vivid yellow, one male and one female pale yellow. Mr. H. paired three males with newly imported green females, and the pale yellow female with an almost blue-yellow male. Unfortunately we did not receive any further report about the result of these efforts.

Meanwhile the yellow Budgerigar has become a constant type, a race, and reversions to the natural type are rare in rational breeding.

A successful breeder of yellow Budgerigars published detailed reports about these birds in *Gef. Welt*, 1904 : " There still remain two principal colour varieties, the bright yellow or brimstone-coloured ones with white wing-feathers and tail-feathers and white-bluish spots at the throat and cheeks, and the dark-yellow birds which also have white tail- and wing-feathers, but darker and more distinct blue spots at the throat and cheeks, and which are a much greater rarity. Feet and bill are identical in the two types, the former being flesh-coloured, the latter, as also the colour of the cere, the same as with the natural bird. The under-surface of the bright yellow ones has mostly a vague greenish hue which appears more intense on the lower part of the back and rump. No green tinge is to be noticed on the dark yellow (sometimes almost yolk-coloured) birds. The latter is the prettier form. Moreover, these birds are always bigger and stronger than the bright yellow ones. When the two types are paired together, they bring forth beautiful offspring. The very young newly-fledged birds show as long as they are still black-eyed the most beautiful yellow colour without any marks, which, however, with advancing years appear more distinctly. I am referring to the dark undulations on the upper surface which is never quite absent in old birds. These markings are, as it were, powdered with yellow and suffused with a feeble green gloss. At the age of about two or three months the young get light pearl-grey eyes (just like the green ones) and at the same time the undulations on the upper surface become noticeable, which were somewhat indistinct at first, just as the blue cere of the male and the greenish-brown one of the female, which in both sexes was almost reddish at first, later on turns a pale blue. An experienced breeder of Budgerigars can infallibly distinguish the sexes at the age of two months only.

"There is also a third colour variety of these Budgerigars, that is an impure greyish-yellow, with the undulations at the upper-surface distinctly present, but of a faded greyish-black. The fore head of these birds is a pale yellow, wing- and tail-feathers are dark. Undersurface and rump are almost greenish with a feeble yellow gloss. The blue spots on the throat and cheeks are present, but pale blue. Thus on the whole they are like the natural bird only much paler and growing yellowish. At first these birds were bred by chance from the green ones, later on they were also obtained as offspring from the yellow ones. They are a reversion to the primitive type. I frequently tried breeding with such birds in order to see the results. Mostly they produced greyish-yellow but never quite green young ones."

Breeding has to be carried out in the same way as with green ones. They also nest in every season. But the yellow Budgerigar is weaker than the green one and must hibernate in a warm room with a temperature of about 60 degrees. Even more than with green birds it is necessary to supply fresh blood when breeding the yellow type: " A very important factor in breeding yellow Budgerigars is the supply of fresh blood, therefore the breeder has to buy periodically, good new birds for breeding; but he must not sell his own breeding couples and continue breeding with the newly acquired couples; that would be useless, he should rather take the male of one couple, the female of another one and replace these by birds of another strain. The birds to be rejected should generally be the oldest or those which did not prove useful for breeding or are of a less pure colour. Further it has to be considered that the new birds should be perfect in all respects. They must be equivalent to one's own breeding-race in all respects, and if possible still better. The purchase of such birds has therefore to be made very cautiously. The best way is to get the birds for that purpose from a reliable breeder of yellow Budgerigars whose name is well known among fanciers or breeders. One should exchange birds with such breeders, as the breeder knows his birds better than the dealer. If, however, one has no other resource than dealers, it is wise not to buy all from the same, but rather from different traders, e.g. the males from one and the females from another. Thus one makes pretty sure that the acquired birds are not brothers and sisters or too nearly related, which otherwise may happen quite easily, as dealers often buy their birds all from the same source. I always went about it in this way when breeding yellow Budgerigars and it always proved right. I was able to avoid the pernicious degeneration I so frequently saw at so many breeders. The breeding of yellow Budgerigars was very profitable in former years when high prices were still paid for these birds."

AILMENTS AND THEIR TREATMENT

Signs of Illness : Loss of vivacity.—Languid, lustreless eyes.—Ruffled plumage, hopping about indolently or sitting motionless with the head bent down.—Suddenly developing tameness.—Wet, dirty or sticky nostrils.—Panting, when not the result of excitement or anxiety.—Producing smacking noises audible in the stillness of the evening.—Puffiness of the breast and belly.—Emaciation.—Deeply sunk, wrinkled and discoloured, or sodden, blistery or inflamed abdomen.—Anal plumage soiled with droppings.—Unnatural condition of droppings. In the ordinary course these consist of two parts, a thick blackish-green and a smaller white. In case of sickness droppings are thin, watery, slimy, greasy, discoloured, evil-smelling.

Treatment of Suspected Illness.—Any bird suspected of disease should be isolated in a cage in a quiet spot. The usual mode of feeding should be continued till one succeeds in diagnosing the disease, though all kinds of stimulating food should be withheld. The Budgerigar suspected of illness only receives white millet. No bathing-water is given to sick Budgerigars.

Diagnosis is often difficult. One must observe the bird and compare its condition with the symptoms described below. If medicines must be used, one should always use the simplest at first. If after conscientious examination one comes to the conclusion that recovery is impossible, one should release the bird from its sufferings by killing it quickly.

Contagious Diseases.—One bird suffering from a contagious disease endangers the whole stock. In case of such disease all the birds must be caught and examined carefully, the sick and suspected being accommodated in special cages. The infected cage or birdroom with all its belongings is cleaned and disinfected. The most efficient disinfectants are boiling water, permanganate of potash, lysol and creolin. If strongly smelling disinfectants are used the cage should be rinsed well, birdroom and aviary must be whitewashed anew, the soil of the aviary must be dug up and renewed. During feeding the utmost precaution is necessary, lest the owner transmits the disease. The apparently healthy birds must always be taken care of at first.

Administering Medicine.—This is a difficult operation. Force should be avoided. Most medicines are administered to the Budgerigar in its drinking-water. As soon as it feels thirsty it will take the offered medicine. Warm drink is given once or twice a day. Before cooling down it should be removed.

Disease of the Respiratory Organs.—Keeping the birds in warm damp air is in many cases a remedy for this. Warm damp air is provided by surrounding the cage with leafy plants and by sprinkling these several times a day with lukewarm water by means of a spray while the room has a temperature of 68 to 86 degrees.

Colds (catarrh of the mucous membrane of the nose and throat).—*Causes :* Draught, icy cold drinking water, sudden change of temperature. Symptoms : Sneezing, yellow slimy discharge from the nostrils gathering in crusts, drooping of the head, bringing up of slime, tears in the eyes. *Remedies :* Daubing with grease, daubing the bill and throat with a solution of chlorate of potassium (1 : 100) ; cleaning the bill and the nostrils with a feather dipped in salted water, daubing with oil, steaming.

Catarrh of the Wind-pipe (Inflammation of the throat, laryngitis).—*Causes :* As above. *Symptoms :* Hoarseness, coughing, accelerated breathing, rattling in the throat, gaping. *Remedies :* In light cases slightly warmed drinking-water, honey and sugar-candy ; daubing the bill well down to the throat, and the nostrils with a solution of salicylic acid in water (1 : 500). Keep in warm damp atmosphere.

Pneumonia.—*Symptoms :* Breathing difficult or short, accompanied by a wheezing sound with wide opened bill, hot breast, dejection, loss of appetite, fever, coughs, expectoration of yellow slime sometimes streaked with blood, smacking noises. *Remedies :* Damp warm atmosphere as above, purified saltpetre (0.02-0.03 gr. in water) to be administered every three hours ; also some nitrate of sodium in the drinking-water and the remedies given for catarrh of the wind-pipe.

Pneumonia caused by fungoid growths mostly attended with inflammation of the intestines is incurable and contagious.

Tuberculosis is mostly the result of hereditary tendencies and appears in the lungs, the liver, the heart, the pericardium, the spleen, the kidneys, the stomach, the ovaries, the intestines, etc., and is always incurable. *Symptoms :* Rapidly losing flesh, sometimes the formation of abscesses in different parts of the body ; also the symptoms of pneumonia.

Diphtheria and Roup.—*Cause :* Vegetable parasites, etc. *Symptoms :* Coughing, sneezing, breathing heavily with open bill, shaking of the head, expectoration of unpleasant-smelling slime, swallowing difficulties, gasping for breath and increasing shortness of breath, snoring and rattling noises, increasing exhaustion, squatting on the floor with drooping wings and closed eyes (nearly always attended with intestinal catarrh, with watery slimy droppings), tremors and thirst. A yellow slimy greasy liquid comes out of the nostrils, consolidating into dark yellow or brownish crusts ; the eye-lids swell and stick together. Duration of the disease 2-3 weeks, but sometimes 60-70 days. Sick birds must be kept apart, as the disease is highly contagious. The curable form is not recognisable by keepers. When the above symptoms show themselves, recovery is impossible.

Diseases of the Stomach and other Digestive Organs.— A weak digestion, frequently in connection with emaciation. *Symptoms :* Loss of appetite, ill-coloured brown, solid or pulpy evil-smelling droppings, laziness, weakness. *Causes :* Unsuitable, bad or too abundant food with the consequent ill effects upon the gall and other digestive liquids. *Remedies :* Light food, little green fodder, a little salt and slightly warmed drinking-water. Strongly recommended is luke-warm red wine, about 3-5 drops in a little drinking-water.—Flatulency (emphysema) has the same causes and occurs mainly in case of young birds. In a light form it is curable by careful piercing of the flat white blistery swelling : the air escapes at slight pressure and then the spot is daubed with warmed oil. Young in the nest are wrapped in soft, loose cotton-wool. The parents of the sick young ones must be given little food. If appearing frequently, put pure hydrochloric acid in the drinking-water (1 : 100).

Diarrhœa.—Generally it is only a symptom of illness. *Signs :* Whitish or yellowish slimy droppings, sticking together of the plumage of the hindquarter, swollen, sometimes inflamed anus. *Remedies :* Instead of drinking-water, thin lukewarm gruel ; no vegetables ; heat ; daubing the abdomen and the inflamed anus with warm oil ; for every bird, daily one drop of tincture of opium in the drinking-water.—In case of dysentery, recognisable by violent pressing of the hind-quarter and rough, slimy, occasionally bloody droppings, one should adminster 2-3 drops castor oil with thin luke-warm gruel, also diluted tincture of rhubarb (3-5 drops in a little drinking-vessel daily) and oil-enemas (see constipation). The sticky hind feathers must be soaked and washed with warm water.

Abdominal Inflammation (inflammation of the stomach and intestines).—*Causes :* Bad or too abundant food, too fresh seeds, wet vegetables, too cold drinking-water, cold draughts. *Symptoms :* The abdomen sags and the bird wags its tail when easing itself ; swollen and red abdomen, protruding sternum ; droppings blackish-green, sour or evil-smelling ; loss of appetite, considerable thirst, sitting exhausted with ruffled feathers and drooping wings. In general the bird is continually near the food-box, rummaging among the seeds but not eating. *Remedies :* Accommodation in an evenly heated room (64-68 degrees) ; no soft food, soaked seeds, vegetables, fruit, etc., daily a drop of opium-solution or red wine in a little lukewarm drinking-water ; rice-water, burnt magnesia (must be mixed with water and offered as a thin gruel) : 1-2 drops of a solution of nitrate of silver (1 : 800) daily. In most cases the bird is lost. Danger of infection is possible.

Typhoid Fever (contagious)—*Cause :* Bacteria, micrococci. *Symptoms :* Violent diarrhœa, with droppings of white-yellow slime, which then become greenish and soil the abdomen, loss of appetite, sitting down exhausted with drooping wings, trembling, sometimes vomiting of a thin greenish fluid, violent thirst, shivering, highly ruffled feathers, death in convulsions. *Preventive measure :* 2 drops of a solution of ferrous sulphate (1 : 500) in the drinking-water. Scarcely curable.

Pyæmia (blood-poisoning by overloading the blood with carbonic acid).—Incurable, rare in case of Budgerigars.

White Diarrhœa.—*Symptoms :* The bird is languid,

depressed, refuses to take its food, weak digestion, droppings slimy, white. *Cause :* Want of food-stuffs containing lime. *Cure :* Supply of food containing lime.

Constipation has different causes. *Symptoms :* Frequent attempts to ease themselves, moving to and fro of the hind-quarters, ruffling of the feathers, dejection, want of appetite. *Remedies :* Mechanical intervention by means of an enema, that is, carefully pushing a pin's head dipped in warmed oil (castor oil and olive oil in equal portions) into the anus, also a water-enema by means of a rubber syringe with thin glass-tube, rounded at the point (difficult to carry out), administering of castor oil with gruel, 1-2 drops once or twice daily.

Emaciation (Phthisis).—Mostly a consequence of illness of the digestive or respiratory organs or any other parts. Cure by ascertaining and removing the different causes.

Obesity.—*Cause :* Neglect and careless feeding. *Signs :* Difficult breathing, coughing, moving heavily, hard or thick droppings, a very full and fat body, languid, wrinkled, inactive skin, bald spots. *Remedies :* Less food, many vegetables ; wide cage ; frequent bathing.

Gout, Gouty Arthritis.—*Causes :* Accumulation of uric acid in the joints. *Symptoms :* Diminishing of appetite, fever, swellings at the joints of the wings and feet ; at first these swellings are hard, red, very warm and painful, then they get soft and contain a liquid mixed with blood and matter ; later on the swellings become hard again and the contents are gelatinous and cheesy ; sometimes after weeks the joint recovers spontaneously, but usually it remains thicker ; in the other case gradual emaciation, anæmia (pale mucous membranes), violent diarrhœa occur and the bird dies from exhaustion. *Preventive measures :* Proper nourishment. *Remedies :* Warmth. When the swelling is inflamed and hot it can be cooled with a solution of vinegar in water or acetate of lead in water, the swelling is wrapped in tow and this is kept wet with the above-mentioned chemicals ; later on the joints are wrapped in warmed wool. If the swelling suppurates an incision has to be made, but on no account too early ; the swelling is then pressed out and daubed with a solution of carbolic acid (1 : 200) ; internally in both cases a dose of a solution of salicylic acid (1 : 500) in water.

Dropsy is very rare. *Symptoms :* At first breathing is rendered difficult, then the body swells and, in extreme cases, distinctly perceptible liquid in the swollen part. Incurable.

Diseases of the Heart, Liver, Spleen and Kidneys are hardly possible to recognise.

Spasms, Epileptic Fits.—*Symptoms :* ¡ The bird suddenly collapses amidst convulsions and flapping of the wings, begins to tremble, staggers, turns its eyes and twists its head, falls and kicks about vehemently. *Causes :* Excitement, fright, anxiety, also obesity ; a cage that is too small, too much heat of the stove or of the sun, unsatisfied sexual instinct, etc. *Remedies :* Change of food, more vegetables and fruit, cool, pure air, change of cage, cold water on the head, purgatives. During the fit one should take the bird in the hand and hold it upright so that it cannot hurt itself. If the fit only happens once, it does not mean much in most cases. But if recurring, remedies must be applied and the causes investigated and removed.

Laying Troubles. Egg-binding.—*Causes :* The female is too young, weakly, tired and ailing, too fat or worn out by too much consecutive brooding ; too high temperature, scarcity of food-stuffs containing lime necessary for the formation of the eggshell ; also disturbance during laying. *Preventive measures :* Avoidance of the causes, proper choice and treatment of females for breeding. *Remedies :* Warmth : the bird is wrapped in cloths, put into the cage near the stove, but not in an overheated place ; steam-baths. It has proved successful to direct a thin jet of cold water on to the abdomen of the bird for several minutes. Introduction of oil into the opening ; destruction of the egg is difficult to carry out and dangerous for the sick Budgerigar.

Apparatus for the application of steam-baths : Different sorts of apparatus for applying steam-baths are for sale. In the illustration below we show an apparatus that every fancier can easily make for himself and which serves its purpose quite well. It is made in the following way : A case made of smoothly planed well-fitting boards with a sliding top, has in the centre of one of the narrow sides a round opening (o). In the interior a ledge (b) is fixed against

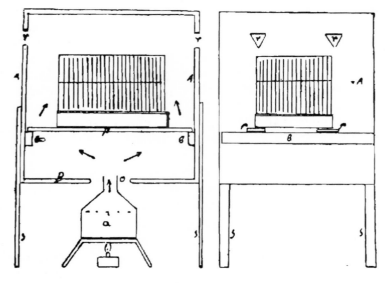

Fig. 31.

the two narrow sides, whereon rest two movable battens (p). The cage with the patient is put on these. The incisions (r) in these two sides serve as outlets for the steam. The four exterior corners of the case rest on four wooden legs (s), which must be high enough for a spirit-kettle (a) to stand underneath, the funnel-shaped top of which enters the case through the round opening (o). The whole is painted with oil-colour. It is advisable to replace the wooden top by a pane of glass.

Parasitic Worms.—The presence of these can hardly be recognised by the layman, therefore remedies are not to be advised. The birds apparently do not suffer much from them.

Rheumatic Complaints and painful paralysis occur in consequence of cold, in particular of draughts. *Remedies :* Rubbing the painful limb with warm oil and wrapping it in a warmed woollen cloth, and keeping the bird in a warm room.

Wounds mostly heal very quickly ; after having washed them with a sponge and clean luke-warm water, one has to clean them with tincture of arnica diluted with water (1 : 25-50) and daub them with oil and carbolic acid (1 : 200).

Fractures likewise heal easily. A simply fractured leg above the joint needs rest for healing. The two ends of the bone can be set right by handling carefully and putting the leg between two pieces of wood, or strips of cardboard ; these are tied with a soft thread and plaster or moderately warm sticky glue is spread over it ; the bird should not move till it has dried up and then be put in a narrow cage with a low, broad perch. After about four weeks the bandage is soaked in water and taken off. In case of simple fractures of the wing one applies cotton-wool over and under the wing after setting it in the natural position and then ties the wing, or better still both wings, tight to the body by means of narrow bandages. Serious fractures with external wounds are treated in the same way as wounds.

Abscesses.—Hard abscesses must be softened by a warm poultice ; a much inflamed (hot and red) swelling must be cooled with a solution of acetate of lead and then softened in the same way by a warm poultice which must often be renewed. A ripe abscess has to be opened up and pressed out, then daubed with carbolic acid (1 : 200) and bandaged if possible. **Atheromas** appear particularly on the head, near the bill, in the region of the eyes ; they are neither hard nor soft, filled with a skinny mass, and grow excessively or go deeper. As long as they are small or lie loose in the skin they can easily be removed by cauterising with nitrate of silver or by ligature, using a strong thin thread. Mostly atheromas result from the corruption of interior liquids. In such cases the bird can only be saved by withdrawal of all unnatural food ; a dose of a solution of salicylic acid (1 : 100 hot water) to be taken for 3 or 6 weeks may be effective.

Swellings of the Conjunctiva, Conjunctivitis, are produced by cold and are an attendant condition of other complaints. *Symptoms :* Tears in the eyes, swelling of the eye-lids, dread of light. *Remedies :* Daubing with luke-warm chloric liquid (1 : 500) or a solution of alum (1 : 500) or sulphate of zinc (1 : 600).—Conjunctivitis or inflammation of the cornea may set in when the eye is hit or bitten. *Remedies :* Cooling with water, daubing with a solution of sulphate of zinc, with opium (1 : 200).

Deformation of the Bill.—If the upper part of the bill projects so far over the under part, that it becomes a hindrance while taking food, it should, after repeated rubbing with warm oil, be cut to its normal length by means of a sharp knife. A split in the horn of the bill is cleaned once a day by means of a brush with warm soap-water and smeared with warm oil.—An apparently normal bill sometimes, after being hurt, begins to grow excessively at the tip, frequently splitting up into fibres. *Cause :*

Faulty nutrition of the horn. It has to be cut to the right size by means of scissors. Natural nourishment, addition of lime, sand, avoiding of soft food are the only remedies.

Foot-diseases.—On the neglected foot of a bird there easily appear under a crust of dirt inflammation, suppuration or ulcers which may lead to inflammation of the joints, mortifying of toes, even loss of the foot. If the inflamed foot is bathed in warm water early, cooled with solution of acetate of lead, the inflamed spots smeared daily with diluted glycerine (1 : 10) and then powdered thickly with the finest starch-flour, a quick recovery is probable.— It is more difficult to remove callosities from which arise sores in the joints or corns. Treatment as mentioned above. *Cause:* Too thin, hard or otherwise defective perches. The corn must be softened by applying warm olive-oil and washing with warm soap-water, then cut out cautiously with a little knife. Further treatment is like that of wounds, and may be supplemented by cauterising with nitrate of silver.—If round the joint of a foot a tough sharp fibre has developed, which by incision has caused inflammation and suppuration, it has to be treated as above and the fibre removed by means of pointed scissors ; the foot heals spontaneously after glycerine-ointment has been spread on it. Foot-sore Budgerigars are given blotting-paper instead of sand as floor-covering of the cage, and comfortable perches.

Overlong toe nails should be cut shorter. It is important not to cut into the quick of the toe. The toe is held against the light in order to see how far the flesh reaches, and is cut considerably below that point.

Crumbling or Splitting of the Toe Nails is caused by over-coddling or illness. The brittle parts may be cut off carefully.

Diseases of the Plumage.—*Causes:* Lack of cleanliness, warm dry air of the room, lack of bathing accommodation, obesity, disease of the gland at the root of the tail, scarcity of feather-forming materials in the food, microscopic parasites of animal or vegetable nature settling in the skin or in the feathers. When the causes are known, the way to recovery is easy. For extermination of the parasites see Chap. viii. Bald spots suddenly appearing are sometimes quickly covered with feathers again if smeared thinly every other day with carbolic acid (1 : 100) or glycerine.

Plucking of their own plumage, gnawing at their own wings and toes is rare among Budgerigars. The causes are neglect, in consequence of which corruption of the blood sets in. Cure very difficult, most likely to be effected gradually by proper care.

Lightning Source UK Ltd.
Milton Keynes UK
UKOW051503121211

183640UK00001B/188/P